Devon and Cornwall

MICHAEL BENNIE

COUNTRYSIDE BOOKS
NEWBURY BERKSHIRE

First published 2005
© Michael Bennie, 2005

All rights reserved
No reproduction permitted without the
prior permission of the publisher:

COUNTRYSIDE BOOKS
3 Catherine Road
Newbury, Berkshire

To view our complete range of books,
please visit us at
www.countrysidebooks.co.uk

ISBN 1 85306 895 0

Designed by Peter Davies, Nautilus Design
Photographs and maps by the author

Produced through MRM Associates Ltd., Reading
Typeset by Mac Style Ltd, Scarborough, N. Yorkshire
Printed by Woolnoough Bookbinding Ltd., Irthlingborough

Contents

Contents

WALKS IN CORNWALL

PUBLISHER'S NOTE

We hope that you obtain considerable enjoyment from this book; great care has been taken in its preparation. However, changes of landlord and actual closures are sadly not uncommon. Likewise, although at the time of publication all routes followed public rights of way or permitted paths, diversion orders can be made and permissions withdrawn.

We cannot, of course, be held responsible for such diversion orders and any inaccuracies in the text which result from these or any other changes to the routes nor any damage which might result from walkers trespassing on private property. We are anxious though that all deatails covering the walks are kept up to date and would therefore welcome information from readers which would be relevant to future editions.

The simple sketch maps that accompany the walks in this book are based on notes made by the author whilst checking out the routes on the ground. They are designed to show you how to reach the start, to point out the main features of the overall circuit and they contain a progression of numbers that relate to the paragraphs of the text.

However, for the benefit of a proper map, we do recommend that you purchase the relevant Ordnance Survey sheet covering your walk. The Ordnance Survey maps are widely available, especially through booksellers and local newsagents.

Introduction

The view from Carvannel Downs, near Portreath.

The south-western peninsula, comprising the counties of Devon and Cornwall, is one of the most rewarding areas for walkers in England, offering an almost endless variety of scenery and walking experiences. These range from the South West Coast Path to the region's three moors, from wooded valleys to open heaths, from stately rivers to rushing streams, from lush farmland to picturesque villages – and always there are the rolling hills to add scale and grandeur to the scene.

In this book I have tried to reflect this variety. There are 20 walks in each county, covering the whole area, from Exmoor in the north to the Lizard in the south, and from the Land's End peninsula in the west to the Dorset border in the east. There are coastal walks, moorland rambles, riverside and woodland meanders, ambles through green lanes and farm fields. They range in length from 4 to 8 miles, and I have graded them easy, moderate or challenging, depending on the difficulty of the terrain and the steepness of any climbs, so that you know what you are letting yourselves in for. Sketch maps are provided, with numbered sections linked to the route descriptions; if you want more detail, I have indicated the relevant Ordnance Survey Explorer map for each walk.

All the routes start and finish at or near a good pub, so that you can relax at the end of your walk and contemplate everything you have done and seen. The choice of pubs and my descriptions of them are, of course, subjective, but I hope you will find them as welcoming as I have. They range from the ancient to the modern, and have been chosen for a variety of reasons: some for their atmosphere, some for their beauty, others for their position or the quality of their food.

Finally, I would like to thank my two 'Last of the Summer Wine' companions, Simon McCandlish and Keith Walter, without whose company, conversation and constructive comment on many of these walks my research would have been not nearly so much fun.

Michael Bennie

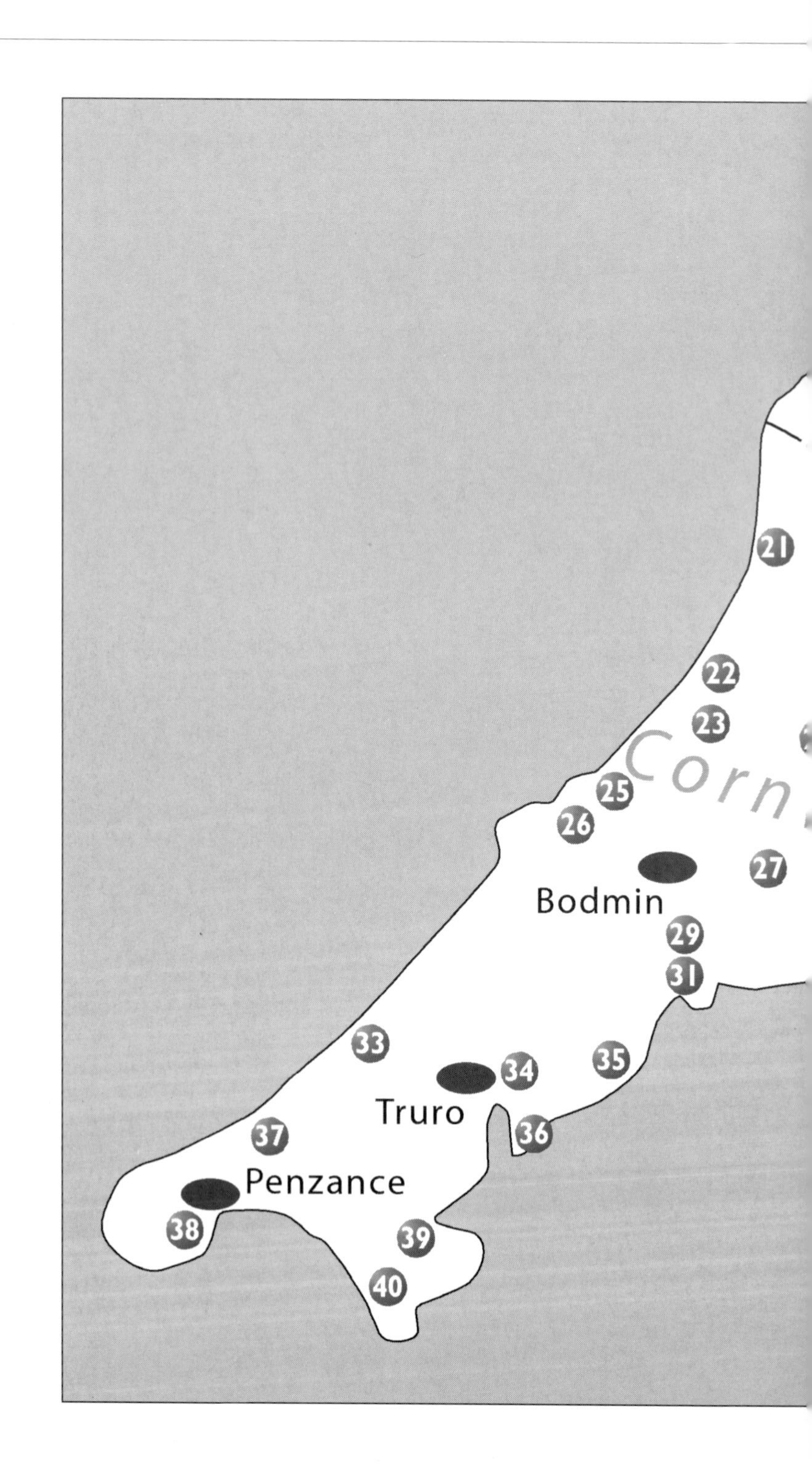
21
22
23
Corn
25
26
27
Bodmin
29
31
33
34
35
Truro
36
37
Penzance
38
39
40

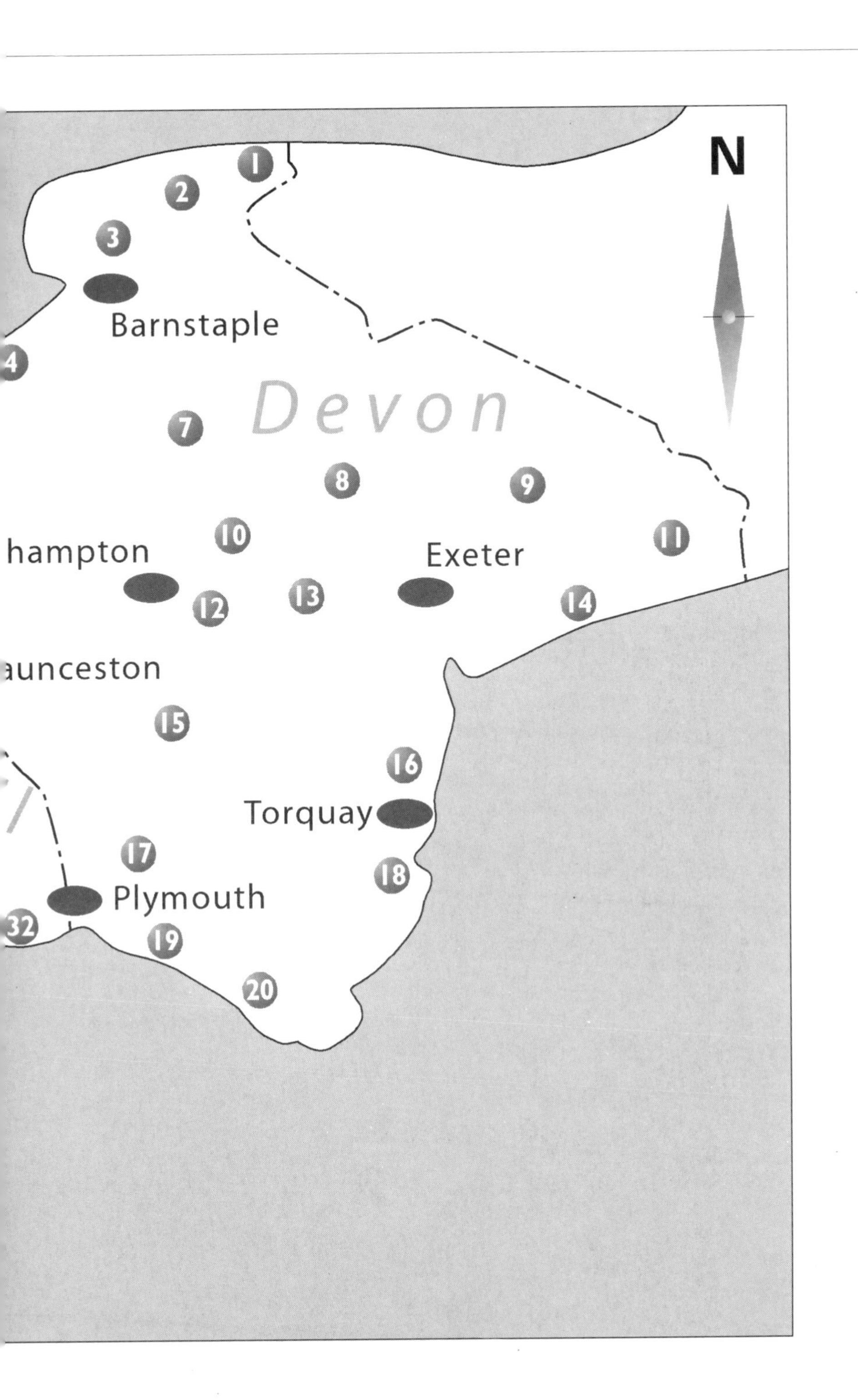
N
Barnstaple
Devon
hampton
Exeter
auncester
Torquay
Plymouth
1
2
3
4
7
8
9
10
11
12
13
14
15
16
17
18
19
20
32

Walk 1 Brendon

The Staghunter Inn

For beauty and variety, this walk is hard to beat. It includes the open spaces of Exmoor, with extensive views in all directions, and a lovely stretch through an old oak wood alongside the splashing, whirling waters of Badgworthy (pronounced 'Badgery') Water. This is also Lorna Doone country, and it is interesting to see the places that inspired R.D. Blackmore's classic novel.

Distance: *7¼ miles*

OS Explorer OL9 Exmoor
GR 767482

A moderate walk, with two steep hills, but along clear tracks and lanes

Starting point: The Staghunter Inn. You may leave your car in the pub car park, but please ask first. Alternatively, there is a public car park by the village hall a short distance beyond the pub.

How to get there: Turn south off the A39 between Lynton and Porlock and follow the signs for Brendon. Just beyond the bridge in the village, turn right to reach the Staghunter.

The oldest part of the **Staghunter Inn** was originally used by the monks of Forde Abbey, which owned the lands locally, when they came to collect their rents. It has been considerably added to since, and now comprises two bars, both with traditional dark beams and large stone fireplaces. The main bar is decorated with delightful local paintings (which are for sale) and with stags' heads and antlers, while the smaller one has hunting and other prints. The menu ranges from soups, ploughman's lunches and baguettes, to steak and Guinness pie and exotic specialities such as Cajun chicken. Local produce is used wherever possible.

Telephone: *01598 741222.*

The Walk

❶ Turn right as you leave the pub, and follow the lane back through the village to the crossroads where you came in. Turn right and climb out of the village. The lane swings right and then, after some more climbing, left. You now get the first of the views, a lovely outlook across the East Lyn valley to the right. About ¾ mile after turning up this lane, you come to a cattle grid and a T-junction. *(1 mile)*

❷ Cross over to a track, where you will see a sign for Dry Bridge and Brendon Common. At the fork a few yards along the track, go straight on. You now get a superb view ahead, to the left and to the right. At the track junction go straight on (signposted to Badgworthy Valley and Malmsmead). Then when the wall and hedge on your left turn left, go straight on up a small hill. As you go, look back for another lovely view, this time across the fields to the coast. Cross a track and then, 300 yards further on, another,

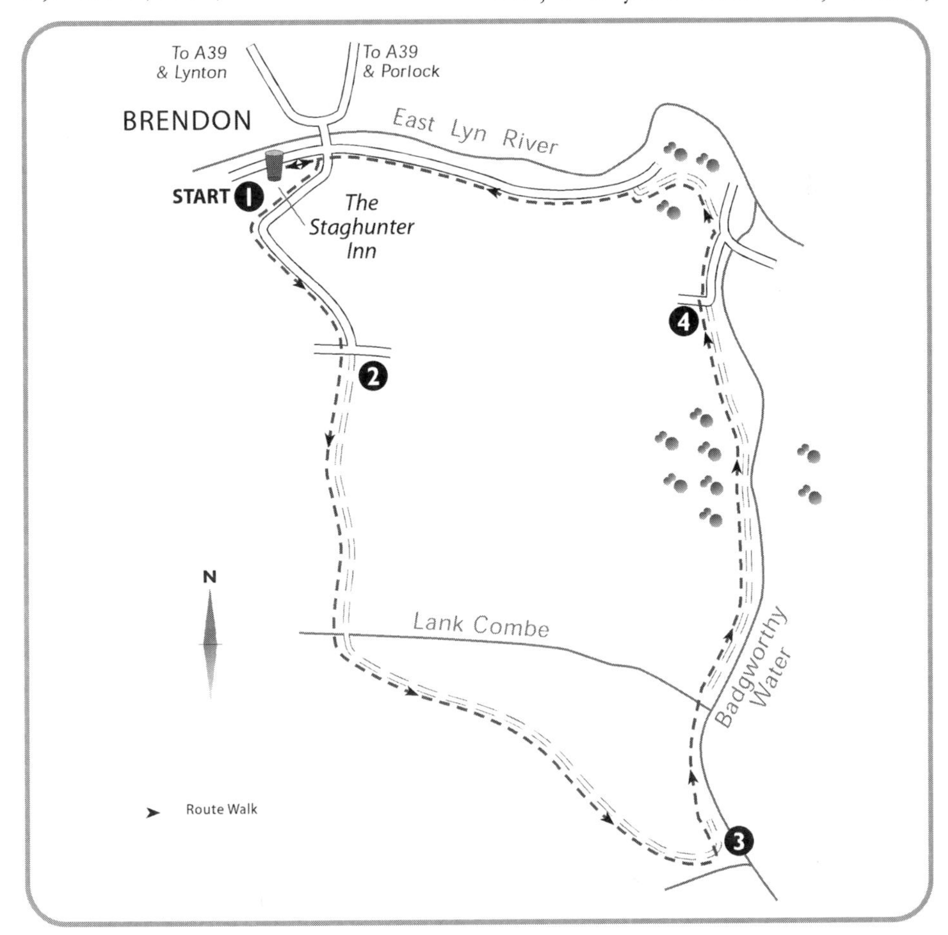

The oak woodlands along Badgworthy Water

much clearer one. Here there is a signpost pointing ahead to Doone Valley. It crosses a stream; the valley to the left is Lank Combe, on which R.D. Blackmore is believed to have based Doone Valley.

Follow the track on the other side as it swings left. It narrows to a path and then almost disappears altogether. It soon reappears, however, and about 3/4 mile after crossing the stream you come to a fence and a gate. Follow the path on the other side, which becomes a grassy track, which in turn gives way to a stony track. It crosses a small stream and continues on the other side. Where it forks a little further on, go left and cross an old wall. Just beyond you will see the remains of a medieval village on your left. Follow the track as it runs parallel to a stream on the right. At the fork, go left (signposted to Cloud Farm and Oare). *(2 3/4 miles)*

❸ The path now runs above and parallel to Badgworthy Water before going down to it and to a wood. You cross a footbridge across Lank Combe. A little way beyond Lank Combe the path joins a track. The track runs for about 1/2 mile through the wood, passing through a gate along the way. It then leaves it and you pass a memorial stone to R.D. Blackmore. At the junction, follow the bridleway sign for Malmsmead. The track leads you away from the river and through a gate. Keep to the track on the other side, along the right-hand side of a field, to reach another gate. The track now runs between fences and swings left and then right, then goes through a gate onto a lane. *(2 miles)*

❹ Go straight on and after about 300 yards you will come to a T-junction; bear left and after a few yards go left through a gate and up a track. There is a bridleway sign pointing to Southern Wood and Brendon Common, but it is on the other side of the gate. The track climbs to another gate leading into a wood and continues to climb on the other side. The track levels off and then starts to descend, and eventually comes out at a lane; bear left. Follow the lane for about a mile to the crossroads on the edge of Brendon. Go straight on to return to the pub. *(1 3/4 miles)*

Date walk completed:

....

Places of Interest Nearby

About 3 miles west of Brendon is Lynmouth, with its spectacular **Glen Lyn Gorge**, containing waterfalls, a water wheel and a water cannon. Telephone: 01598 752529. Also at Lynmouth is the **Exmoor Brass Rubbing Centre**, which offers instruction in how to do brass rubbing, plus examples to work on. Telephone: 01598 752529.

Parracombe

The Fox and Goose Inn

Parracombe is a charming little village set in delightful surroundings, and on this lovely walk you have the opportunity to explore both. The route takes you down the pretty, densely wooded valley of the Heddon River and then branches off along the equally pretty Trentishoe Coombe. The return to Parracombe is through more woodland and along farm paths and quiet lanes, with a superb viewpoint along the way.

Distance: *6½ miles*

OS Explorer OL9 Exmoor
GR 667448 (pub); GR 670450 (car park)

A challenging walk with some steep hills

Starting point: The free car park at the north-eastern end of the village. The pub car park is very small, and walkers are asked not to leave their cars there while they walk.

How to get there: Parracombe is just off the A39 between Blackmoor Gate and Lynton. Approached from Lynton, the car park is on the left about ¼ mile from the main road with the pub further down on the right. From Blackmoor Gate you will come to the pub first with the car park on through the village.

The bar of the pretty 18th-century **Fox and Goose Inn** is panelled and decorated with old photographs, brass dishes and deer antlers, and has delightful Victorian stained-glass light shades. There is also a little snug, a family room and a light and airy dining room. At the back is a patio beside the infant Heddon River. The pub is renowned for its fish, meat and game, all of which are local. The menu ranges from soup and pâté to steak, lobster and a range of vegetarian dishes – not forgetting the award-winning steak and seaweed pie.

Telephone: 01598 763239.

The Walk

❶ Turn right out of the car park and follow the lane as it climbs out of the village. After a little under 1/4 mile, as the lane bends right to join the main road, you will see a public footpath sign on the left pointing to Higher Bodley. Turn up a track and go through a gate. Head for the far right-hand corner of the field beyond. Cross a stile and keep to the right of a short field to another. Cut across the next field, following the clear path. This leads to a gate; keep to the left of the next field to a gate leading onto a lane. Turn right and at the T-junction turn left. Descend the lane for 1/4 mile and take the signed public footpath on the left through a gate to Bumsley Mill. *(3/4 mile)*

❷ Follow this track to a gate. Keep to the right of the field beyond to another gate. Follow the right-hand fence in the next field as it curves left, and at the end follow the bottom fence to the left above some trees to reach a gate. Go through and follow the path steeply down among the trees. Near the bottom go through a gate and follow the path down to a surfaced drive; turn sharp right. Follow the drive through the wood. After about 300 yards go left down a footpath (signed), cross the river and turn right along a path on the other side. Shortly, cross another bridge on the right and rejoin the drive. Turn left at the lane. After 1/4 mile, go straight on through a gate, following the sign for the Hunter's Inn and Heale. *(1 1/4 miles)*

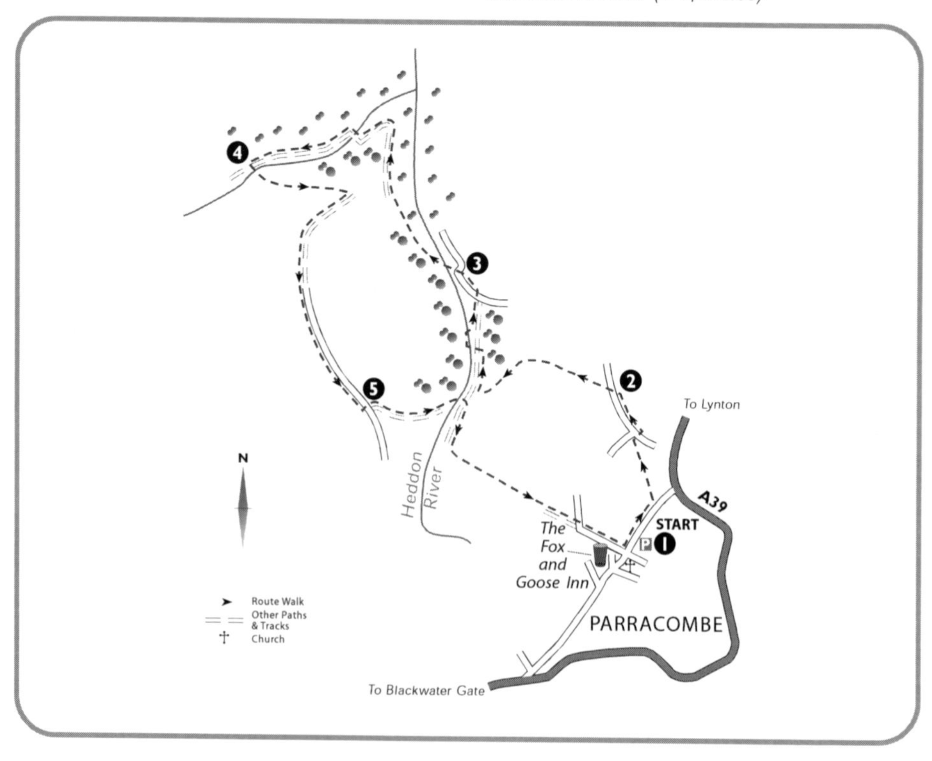

❸ Keep to the left of a field to reach a gate and a footbridge. Turn right on the other side and go through another gate. You now encounter the first of the hills. Ignore the steps going down on the right and carry on climbing. You come out onto a broad grassy track; cross over and continue to climb. At the top of the wood go through a gate and turn right along the wood bank. Go through a gate and bear left to a track; follow it along the edge of the wood and then down among the trees. At the bottom of the valley there is a junction of four tracks; go half right (not sharp right), following the sign for Rhydda Bank Corner. Cross a footbridge and turn left along another track (signposted to Rhydda Bank Corner and Trentishoe Mill). After 1/4 mile you come to a junction; carry on along the main track (signposted to Heale and Trentishoe Mill). After another 1/4 mile there is another junction, with a path leading left to Parracombe and Heale. *(1 1/2 miles)*

❹ Follow this path down to the stream and cross a footbridge and a stile. Turn left and walk up through the wood, following the valley of a small rivulet. After a while you cross it and continue on the other side. This is the second of the steep climbs. Go through a gate and along a track above the valley. It leaves the wood and continues to climb. Towards the top go left at a fork. Follow the path and at a gateway, bear right along a wall. You will come out at a stile leading onto a track. Turn right (signposted to Heale). The track leads through a farm to a lane. At the top, there is a superb view. After about 3/4 mile, as the lane curves right, take the left-hand track. *(1 1/4 miles)*

❺ The track leads to a gate onto a surfaced drive. Follow it down a hill, and when it curves right to a house go straight on to a gate. Follow the path on the other side down through a wood towards the Heddon River again. After 200 yards look out for a small cleared area with a narrow path going sharp right; it is not very clear and there is no waymark. Follow it down to the river and a stone stile followed by a footbridge. Turn left along a track and after a few yards sharp right along another track (signposted to Parracombe). When you come to a junction bear right and follow a grassy track until it turns right into a field. Go straight on along a path, which takes you up to a gate. Keep to the right of four fields separated by gates, and then one more gate takes you onto a green lane. Follow that down to yet another gate and onto a lane; turn right. After 1/4 mile this lane brings you out at a T-junction in Parracombe; turn left to return to the car park and right to the pub. *(1 3/4 miles)*

Date walk completed:

....

Places of Interest Nearby

About 4 miles south of Parracombe is the **Exmoor Zoo**. Telephone: 01598 763352. **Glen Lyn Gorge** is 5 miles to the east is Lynmouth. Telephone: 01598 752529.

Walk 3 West Down

The Crown Inn

Green lanes and farm tracks provide ideal habitats for a wide range of flora and fauna, and this corner of North Devon boasts a number of extremely attractive ones, some of which we follow on this ramble. Hedgerow flowers are the main attraction in season, but there is also a pretty stretch of woodland and some lovely views.

Distance: *$5\frac{3}{4}$ miles*

OS Explorer 139 Bideford, Ilfracombe and Barnstaple
GR 515411

A moderate walk; the going is easy but there are a few hills to climb

Starting point: The Crown Inn. The pub car park is very small, so please do not leave cars there while walking. There is plenty of parking around the square and in the roads through the village.

How to get there: West Down is a mile east of the A361 between Ilfracombe and Braunton, and is signposted from it. The pub is in the centre of the village.

The **Crown Inn** is an attractive pub, converted from three 17th-century cottages. The main bar is a cosy, stone-walled room with padded benches and a log fire at one end in winter. Beyond that is a snug eating area, also with stone walls. There is also what they call the pool bar, which has a pool table, dartboard and fruit machine. At the back is a beautiful long, sheltered garden. A good selection of bar food is available, ranging from sandwiches, jacket potatoes and large salad baguettes to chicken, scampi and a number of daily specials. There is a separate evening menu.

Telephone: 01271 862790.

The Walk

❶ Turn right as you leave the pub, and then almost immediately left. Pass the post office on the right and the church on the left. Immediately opposite the church, just before a house called Church Pool House, turn right along a public footpath between a wooden fence and a wall. Once past the houses you go through a kissing-gate onto a track, then through another kissing-gate onto a lane. Turn right and follow the lane for 100 yards to a track on the left with a public footpath sign. Turn down it. The track takes you down between high banks and past a house. You go through a kissing-gate and the track bends to the right. Go through another gate, and you get a view up a pretty wooded valley. There are wild flowers on either side in season, and in summer the foxgloves are particularly fine. When the track forks at a gate, go left. At the next fork, also by a gate, bear right.

The track climbs and towards the top of the hill you get a good view of the undulating farmland half left. Go through a kissing-gate and follow the track downhill. It swings left and as it does so you will see a kissing-gate on the right,

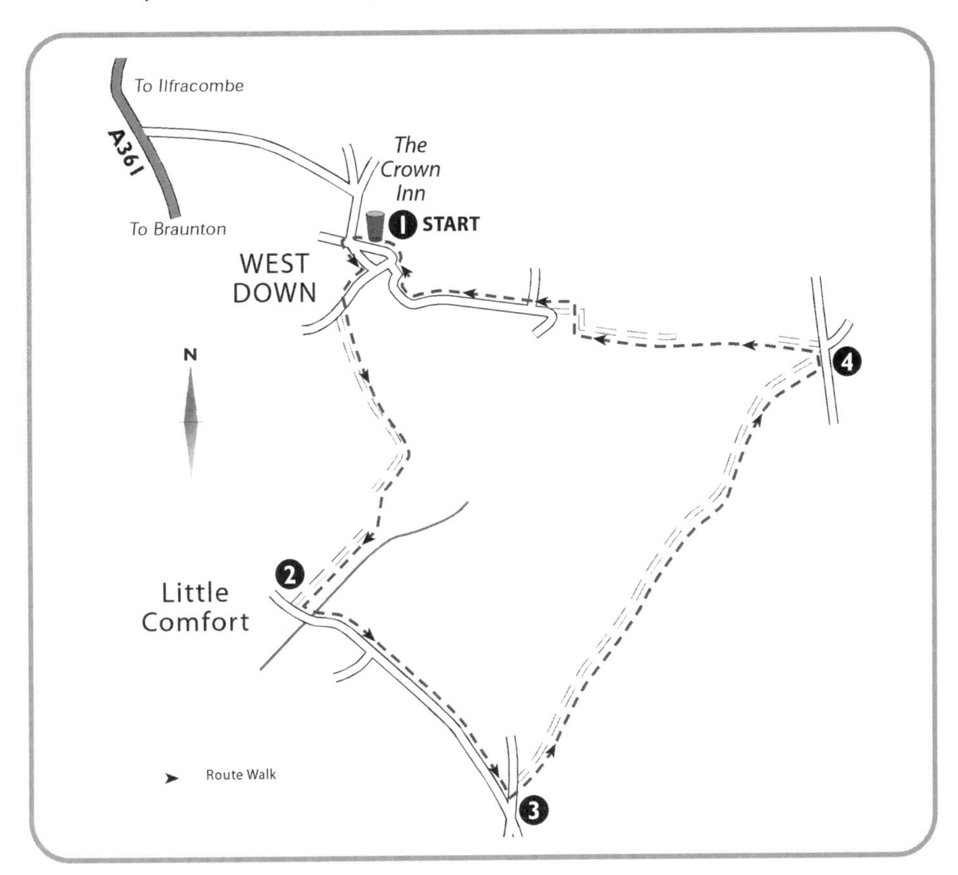

with an arrow pointing to Little Comfort. Go through and down the field on the other side, and into a wood. Go through another kissing-gate at the bottom onto another path; bear right. You are now skirting the lower edge of the wood, with a meadow and stream on your left. Go through yet another kissing-gate and bear right into a field. Ignore the paths leading down to the stream and stay on the track above it. You emerge onto a much clearer track; bear left, go through a gate and out onto a lane. *(1½ miles)*

❷ Turn left past Little Comfort Farm and cross the stream. The lane swings left, then right and left again, climbing as it does so. As it begins to level off at the top you come to a junction; go straight on (signposted to Marwood). As you go, look over to your right for another good view over the hills and fields. The lane continues to climb, but more gently now. As you come over the brow of the hill, another panorama opens up ahead of you, and you come to a crossroads. *(1 mile)*

❸ Turn left (signposted to Fullabrook). After 200 yards, as the lane curves to the left, turn right along a track. The foxgloves along the banks on either side here form a purple mass in summer. When the main track swings left into a field after about ½ mile, go straight on along a green lane. This takes you between banks, walls and hedges for about 600 yards and emerges onto another track for a short distance. When that track also swings left into a field, go straight on along the green lane. You then come out onto another broad track, which leads to a lane. *(1¾ miles)*

❹ Just before you reach the lane, turn sharp left onto another green lane, following the public footpath sign. After a while it emerges into a field. You get a lovely view down the valley ahead of you now. At the end of the field you join another green lane, which runs between hedges for about 500 yards. When you come to a gate, turn right, following the public footpath sign, cross two stiles and bear left up another green lane, climbing as you go.

This emerges onto a lane; go straight on, continuing to climb. At the junction, go straight on (signposted to West Down). Soon you get a pretty view half right across the village. After 600 yards, as the lane begins to swing left, turn off to the right up some steps and across a stile, following the public footpath sign. Cross a small field to another stile and keep to the right of the next field to a stone stile. This leads you into a lane; go straight on. At the junction go right, and at the next follow the lane round to the left. Soon you will see the Crown Inn on your right. *(1½ miles)*

Date walk completed:

....

Places of Interest Nearby

About 3 miles north of West Down is the **Mullacott Miniature Pony and Shire Horse Centre.** Telephone: 01271 866877. A little further, about 4 miles to the west of the village is **Once Upon a Time**, a theme park for young children. Telephone: 01271 867474.

Abbotsham 4 Walk

The Thatched Inn

This is a lovely walk, with a great deal of variety. You go out along quiet roadways, flower-fringed in summer, and green lanes to the South West Coast Path. You then follow this path for $1\frac{1}{2}$ miles, with outstanding views in both directions, before returning to Abbotsham along farm paths and more pretty lanes.

Distance: 5 miles

OS Explorer 139 Bideford, Ilfracombe and Barnstaple
GR 424266

A fairly easy walk with few climbs

Starting point: The Thatched Inn. The pub car park is very small, so walkers are asked to park on the road, where there is generally plenty of space.

How to get there: Turn west off the A39 Bideford to Bude road just outside Bideford, following the signs for Abbotsham. Turn west again off the main road through the village (right if you are approaching from the Bideford direction, left from the Bude side) to reach the pub.

The **Thatched Inn** is an attractive hostelry which dates back to the 15th century. It is a very welcoming place, with thick stone walls, exposed beams and warming gas fires in the impressive fireplaces in winter. There is a pretty beer garden. The landlord prides himself on his real ales, and the seasonal menu is equally impressive. The fare ranges from pasties, sandwiches and jacket potatoes to steaks, fish and vegetarian main courses, and most of it is home-made.

Telephone: 01237 471321.

The Walk

❶ Turn right from the pub and take the first turning on the right, which is Pump Lane. At the next junction bear right, and at the edge of the village follow the lane round to the right. Where it turns left again, go straight on along a green lane (signposted as unsuitable for motors). It crosses a stream, just beyond which is a stretch that can be rather wet after rain. It climbs out of the valley; as it does so, look back for a good view over the village. *(½ mile)*

❷ You emerge onto a lane; turn left and almost immediately right (signposted to Cornborough). As you do so, look to the left for a superb view out to sea. A lovely variety of flowers can be seen in the hedgerow along here in season. The lane climbs and at the top you get another splendid view to the sea on the left and across the rolling farmland on the right.

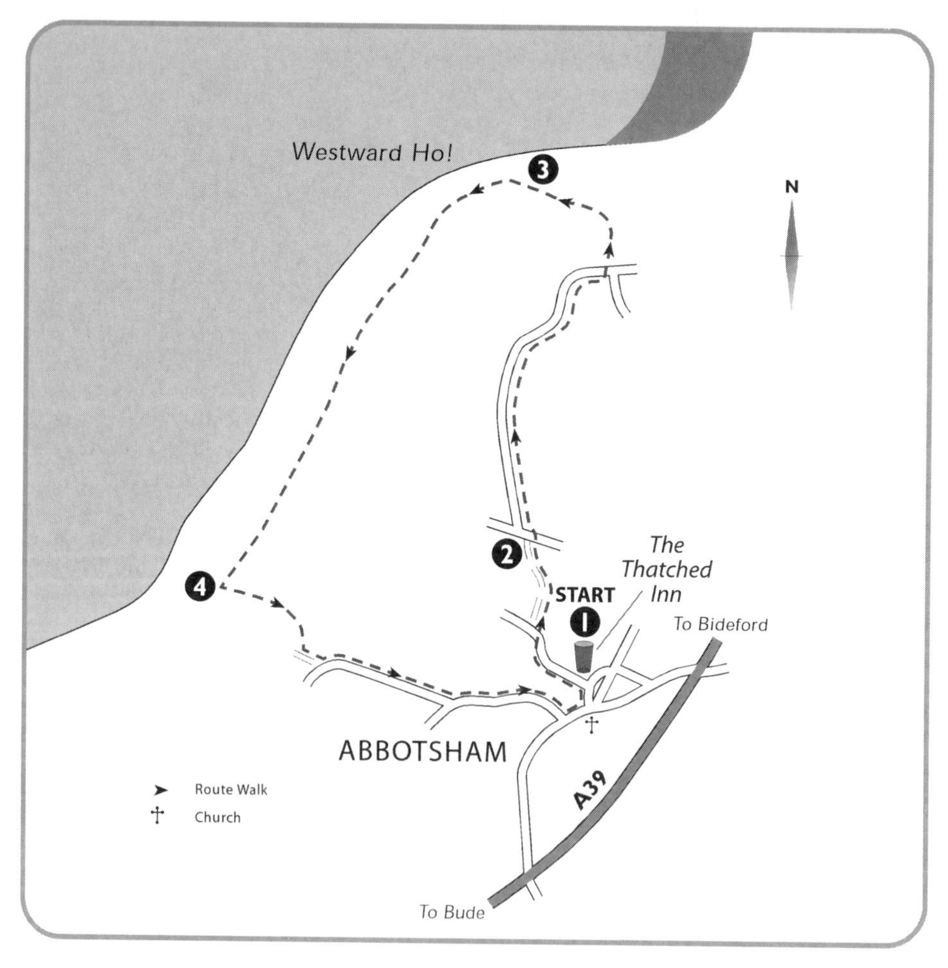

The pebble beach at Cornborough

You pass a heliport on your left and about 1/4 mile later the lane turns sharply to the right. You pass the entrance to an estate called Highcliffe Park, and a short distance beyond it there is a lane going off to the right, with a public footpath opposite it, signposted to Westward Ho! Go through a gate and you will see the long beach at Westward Ho! ahead of you. The path runs between houses and you will come to a junction. Go straight on, and you will see Lundy ahead of you. The path takes you behind a caravan park to join the South West Coast Path. *(1 1/2 miles)*

❸ Follow this broad path alongside the rocky shoreline. After a while you cross a V-stile and another magnificent panorama opens up ahead of you, round to Clovelly and Hartland Point. Keep following the Coast Path as it runs along this lovely stretch of coast. The area around you is a mass of yellow gorse and white blackthorn in late spring. You pass a footpath leading left to Abbotsham; carry straight on along the Coast Path. You go through a gate and then across a stile, and about 1/2 mile after the first footpath you will cross a small footbridge; on the other side you will find another footpath to Abbotsham on the left; take that. *(1 1/2 miles)*

❹ After a short distance you cross a stile into a field; keep to the left and at the end bear right to another stile. This takes you onto a path between fences. At the end cross another stile onto a farm drive and turn left. After a few yards there is a junction; go straight on. After a little under 1/2 mile you will come to a T-junction; turn left (signposted to Abbotsham and Bideford). At the next T-junction turn left, and then turn left again opposite the church to return to the pub. *(1 1/2 miles)*

Date walk completed:

....

Place of Interest Nearby

Just outside Abbotsham is **The Big Sheep**, a farm park which features a range of attractions, including sheep racing. Telephone: 01237 472366.

Walk 5 Horns Cross

The Coach and Horses Inn

Woods are the main feature of this walk – there is a small one on the outward leg and a long stretch of almost 2 miles along the Coast Path on the way back. However, there are also green lanes, farm tracks and streamside paths to add a different perspective, and one or two viewpoints along the way. There are a few stiff climbs, but on the other hand you will enjoy a breathtaking variety of scenery and flora.

Distance: *5¾ miles*

OS Explorer 126 Clovelly and Hartland GR 381232

A fairly challenging walk, with some steep hills and the occasional bit of rough terrain

Starting point: The Coach & Horses. The landlord usually has no objection to customers leaving their cars in the car park while they walk, as long as they ask. Otherwise there is room for one car in the lane that runs south opposite the pub and also a lay-by on the A39 just outside Horns Cross on the Bideford side.

How to get there: Horns Cross is on the A39 between Bideford and Bude, and the pub is on the main road.

Built in the 17th century, the **Coach & Horses** is believed to have been a coaching inn. It is a small pub, very cosy and welcoming. There is just the one main room, which is panelled and decorated with old photographs, and has a large stone fireplace with a wood-burning stove. Across the car park, however, is a children's room with games. The menu ranges from toasted sandwiches to steaks and their speciality beef and Guinness pie. There is also a variety of home-made daily specials. Local produce is used where possible – all the meat, for example, is local.

Telephone: *01237 451214.*

The Walk

❶ Cross the main road to the lane that runs south out of the village. After 150 yards, where it turns sharp left, go right along a concrete track. At the end follow it round to the left. When it turns left into a farmyard, go straight on along an unsurfaced track. When this swings right into a field, go straight on along a green lane. At the end of that cross a stile and keep to the left of the field beyond. Go down the field and follow the boundary round to the right, alongside a wood. At the end cross a stile and go down some steps. Keep to the right for a few yards to another stile. Keep to the right again to a gate. *(3/4 mile)*

❷ On the other side of the gate is a track; bear right and go through another gate at the end. Keep right in the field beyond, and at the end go through another gate. On the other side bear slightly right across another field. After 150 yards or so you will come to a stile in the fence on the right just where a bank comes up from the valley on the left. Cross it and turn left to follow the left-hand boundary. Follow this down to the left to a pretty wood. As you enter the wood look for a path that swings left down to a stream; do not follow the broader path which runs parallel to the stream. Cross a stile and a footbridge at the bottom and follow the green lane that runs up the other side.

After 50 yards you come to a junction; turn right and follow a new green lane. It emerges onto a lane; turn left. After 200 yards you come to a crossroads; turn right (signposted to Broad Parkham). The lane winds and climbs steeply, and after 1/4 mile bends left. Turn right along a track. *(3/4 mile)*

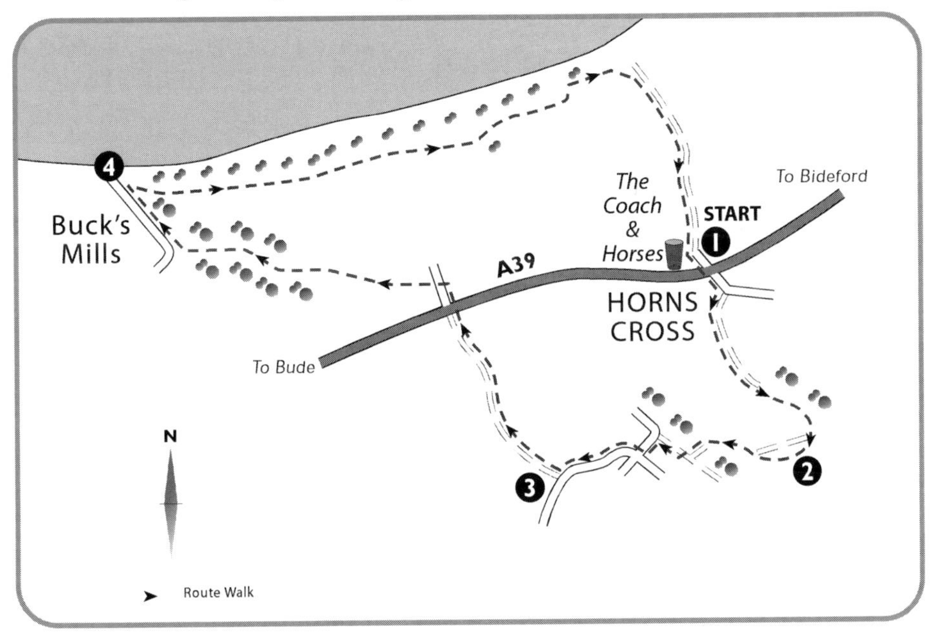

❸ The track passes a farmyard, still climbing and winding, and then narrows to a pretty green lane, flower-filled in summer. At the top of the climb this swings to the right and then to the left and you get a magnificent view on the right before the hedges close in again. Where the green lane forks, go right. You emerge onto a surfaced track by some houses; follow it to the main road and cross to a lane. After 100 yards you will see a public footpath sign on the left. Leave the lane here, cross a stile and keep to the right of the field on the other side. Go through a gate at the end and keep to the right again. At the end of that field go through a gate on the right and up a grassy track.

Go left just beyond a house, following the footpath sign to take a concrete track into a farmyard. Just before you come to a gate bear right up a ramp, following the yellow waymark. Go through a small gate and a short path leads you to a stile; cross it and keep to the left of a field. Where the hedge turns left go straight on to enter a wood. The path runs along the hillside, with the delightful wood stretching down to a stream on the left and also up the slope on the right. It then goes down into the valley and crosses a small footbridge before following the stream down the valley. It is idyllic along here, with the stream tumbling down beside you and the thick undergrowth all around. All too soon you emerge past a house and turn left through an arch. Cross a footbridge to join a lane. Turn right and follow the lane down to the settlement of Buck's Mills. *(1¾ miles)*

❹ Shortly before you get to the bottom, you will see a Coast Path sign pointing to the right. Follow it past some houses and then swing left and right up some steps. The path zigzags steeply up a hill and through a wood above Buck's Mills, with steps from time to time to make the going a bit easier. Near the top the path forks; go left, following the Coast Path sign.

The path now thankfully begins to descend. You now skirt the top of a wood, with occasional glimpses of the coastline through the trees below you. After about ¾ mile you come to a path junction; go straight on, following the Coast Path sign again. After another mile or so the path emerges onto a track. Turn right and follow it up a hill. It is a long and steady climb to a gate leading onto a lane. Turn left to return to Horns Cross and the pub. *(2½ miles)*

Date walk completed:

....

Places of Interest Nearby
Four miles along the A39 towards Clovelly is **The Milky Way**, a farm and adventure park which also has a bird of prey centre. Telephone: 01237 431255.

Welcombe

The Old Smithy Inn

Despite some steep hills, this is a beautifully varied walk. There is a lovely woodland path above and through the Marsland Valley Nature Reserve, a short coastal stretch with magnificent views, fascinating rock features around Welcombe Mouth, and lanes and tracks that are fringed by flower-filled hedgebanks for much of the year.

Distance: *6 miles*

OS Explorer 126 Clovelly and Hartland GR 231179

A challenging walk, with some steep climbs

Starting point: The Old Smithy Inn. Customers may leave their cars in the car park while they walk.

How to get there: Turn west off the A39 Bude to Bideford road just north of the Devon/Cornwall border, following the sign for Welcombe. After a little over a mile, where the lane forks, follow the main lane to the left. After a further ¾ mile, turn right by a group of houses; the pub is down there.

The attractive thatched **Old Smithy Inn** was occupied by the local blacksmith until the 1960s, although the actual smithy was next door. It comprises a single bar, with stone fireplaces at each end. Thick walls and dark beams attest to its age – probably about 400 years. There is also a pretty garden. The menu is very imaginative, and changes every day. Fresh local produce is used wherever possible, and the fish is a particular speciality. For those who just want a snack, there is a range of sandwiches and pizzas.

Telephone: 01288 331305.

The Walk

❶ Turn right from the pub entrance and go down to a small lane; turn right again. After about 200 yards, as the lane begins to descend, turn right into a track, marked as unsuitable for motors. When it swings left into a field, go straight on along a green lane. After a while the green lane joins another track, which becomes a surfaced lane. When you reach a crossroads, turn right. Follow this lane for about 250 yards to a T-junction; turn left. *(3/4 mile)*

❷ After another 250 yards you will see a public footpath sign on the right, pointing over a field. Cross a stile and bear slightly left across the field to another. This is quickly followed by a footbridge and then another stile. Cut across the next field to a set of double gates. Cross a track and follow a rough path to a gate leading into a farmyard. Go through to a lane and turn right. The lane swings sharply right and then left, and then ends. *(3/4 mile)*

❸ Carry on down a track, and at the fork after a few yards go straight on, following the bridleway sign. The track leads down into a lovely wood and then swings sharp left. Go straight on here, following the bridleway sign. You descend further into the wood between banks of flowers. After 3/4 mile you cross a footbridge. On the other side is a footpath going right; ignore it and carry on along the bridleway. It now begins to climb steadily and joins a track; turn left. The track descends steeply to cross Marsland Water and then becomes a lane. *(1 mile)*

❹ Shortly afterwards, and just before it bends to the left, turn right down a drive. Pass a couple of cottages and cross Marsland Water again. Just before the gate of a house called Tall Trees, turn left along a footpath alongside Marsland Water. Cross a stile and continue through the wood on the other side. This is another lovely stretch, with the river on your left and the dense woodland all around. Soon the path climbs away from the river. Go right at a fork and continue climbing. You come out at a clearing with a superb view down the wooded valley to the coast. You then cross a stile and

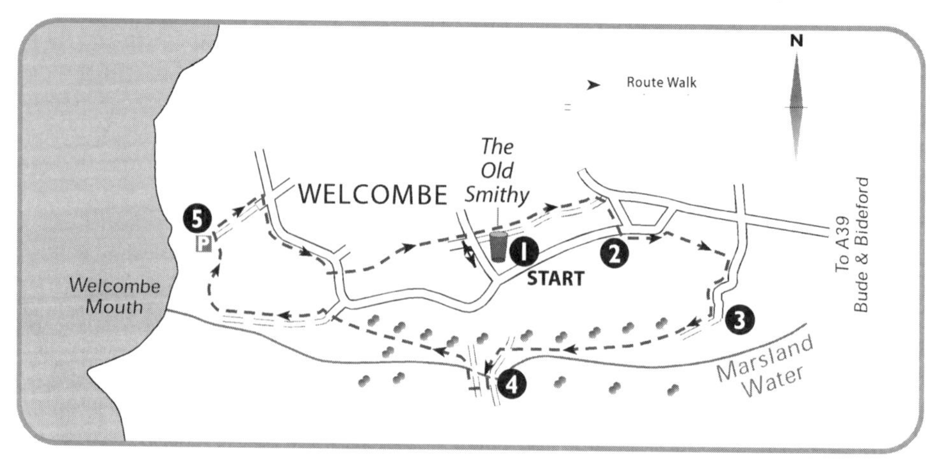

Fascinating rock formations at Welcombe Mouth

follow a path among gorse and bracken to a gate into a lane. Turn left and at the junction go straight on, following the footpath sign. This leads you along a track which descends to Marsland Mouth.

When you reach a house, go up some steps to the right, following the footpath sign. Go through a kissing-gate and then a little later cross a stile. You are now on the Coast Path; turn right up some steps. There is a steep climb, with steps, to get over the headland, but at the top there is a hut where you can rest and enjoy the view. There is then just a short climb up the rest of the hill to a stile. Keep to the right of the field beyond, with a good view of Knap Head. Ignore the footpath on your right and cut across to a stile marked with the Coast Path acorn. On the other side the path descends steeply to Welcombe Mouth. *(1½ miles)*

5 Turn sharp right to follow the track away from the Welcombe Mouth car park. It becomes a surfaced lane and you come to a crossroads; turn sharp right (signposted to Hartland and Bude). After about 700 yards of climbing you come to a junction; go straight on, and about 100 yards beyond it, as the lane swings right, go left into the drive of Mead Barn Cottage. Go through a holiday complex and at the end turn right and then left up some steps and across a stile into a field. Bear left to reach the far left-hand corner and cross another stile. Keep to the left again and at the end of that field you will find another stile on the left. Cross it into a green lane and follow that for 200 yards or so until it emerges onto the lane you came out on. Turn right, and you will find the pub on your left after another 200 yards. *(2 miles)*

Date walk completed:

....

Places of Interest Nearby

Four miles south of Welcombe, near Morwenstow, is the **Killarney Springs Family Park** which offers water and farm attractions. Telephone: 01288 331475. At Kilkhampton, 6 miles to the south, you will find **Brocklands Adventure Park**, with a variety of rides and activities. Telephone: 01288 321920.

Walk 7 # Chittlehamholt

The Exeter Inn

Beautiful views and pretty lanes are the main features of this delightful walk, with colour and interest throughout the year – from spring flowers to autumn leaves. The scenery in this hidden corner of Devon, tucked between the valleys of the Taw and the Mole, can be quite breathtakingly lovely – rolling fields, wooded slopes, green lanes and ancient hedgerows – and this route enables you to appreciate it to the full.

Distance:* *6 miles

OS Explorer 127 South Molton and Chulmleigh
GR 650209

A moderate walk along easy paths and lanes, with one or two fairly stiff climbs

Starting point: The Exeter Inn. The landlord has no objection to customers leaving their cars in the pub car park while walking (provided they ask), but it is not very big, so you may prefer to park in the village hall car park 200 yards down the road to the south.

How to get there: Turn west off the B3226 South Molton to Crediton road and follow the signs.

Built in the 15th century and licensed in the 18th, the welcoming, thatched **Exeter Inn** once served the packhorse trains that plied the route from Barnstaple to Exeter. The stone floor around the bar gives way to carpeting in the other areas, which comprise a comfortable lounge, a family area, and a snug little restaurant. There are tables outside in the front. The low beams are decorated with an interesting collection of matchboxes and books, and there are stone fireplaces. All the food is home-cooked and ranges from soups and light meals to popular specials such as steak and Guinness pie and beef stroganoff.

Telephone: *01769 540281.*

The Walk

❶ Whether you are starting from the pub or the village hall car park, turn right and follow the lane out of the village. After a little under ³/₄ mile turn right down another lane (signposted to Clapworthy and South Molton). After a while the lane descends quite steeply and you get a good view of the wooded hills ahead of you. After ³/₄ mile the lane joins the B3226. *(1¹/₂ miles)*

❷ Turn left (signposted to South Molton). After 300 yards you will see a public bridleway sign pointing left. Follow it to two gates; go through the right-hand one. Climb steeply up the left of the field beyond and at the top go left through a gate and keep to the right of the next field. At the top go through another gate onto a green lane. As you go, look back for a very good view of the undulating farmland behind you. About 600 yards after joining the green lane you come to a farm, with the interesting little Satterleigh church on the left. It is a tiny 15th-century building with a weatherboard bellcote. Unfortunately it is now in need of some repair, but it is worth pausing to

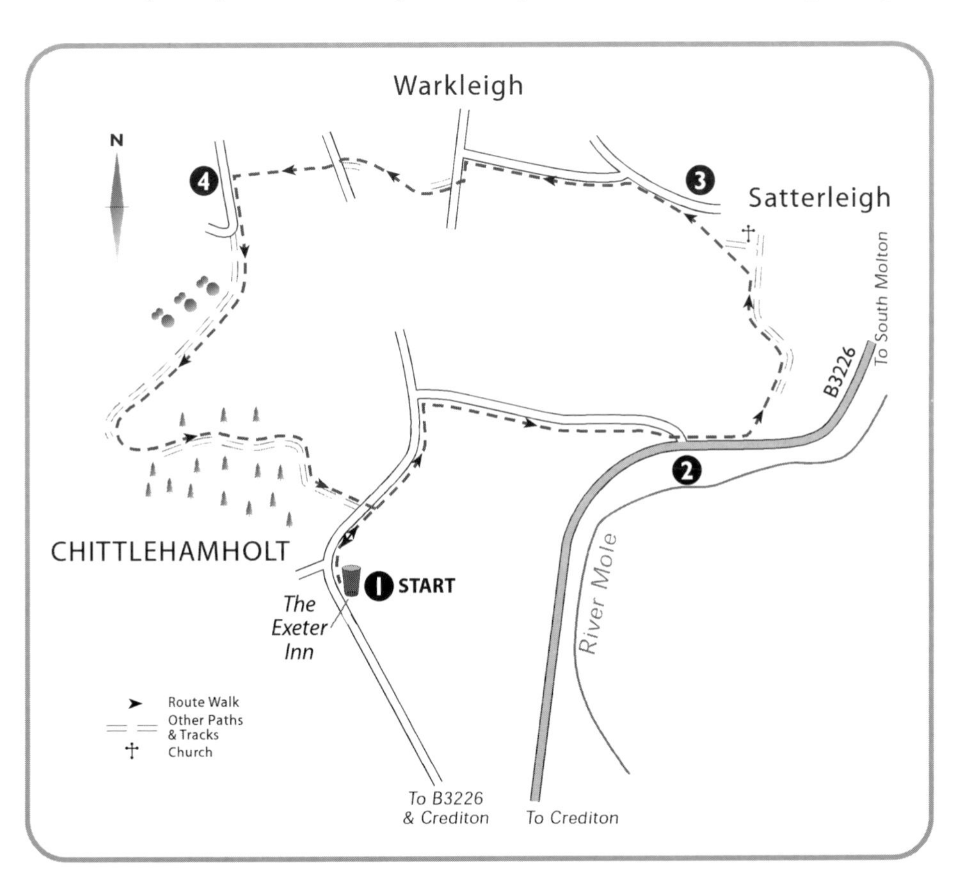

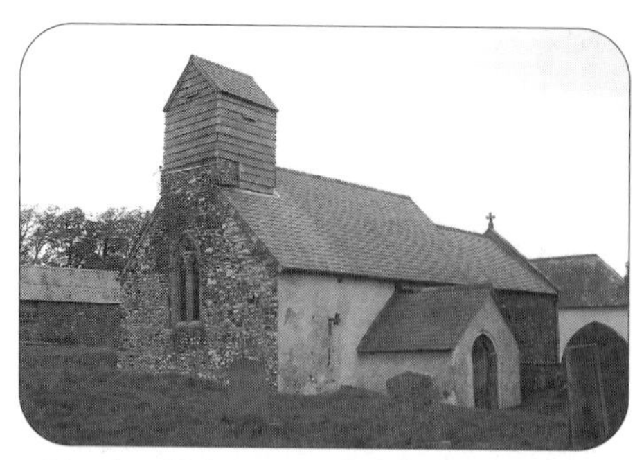

The tiny 15th-century church at Satterleigh

appreciate it and the little churchyard in which it is set. Turn left up a track just before you reach it, and at the end bear right through a gate. Keep to the left of the field on the other side to reach a stile. *(1 mile)*

❸ Turn left in the lane beyond, and after a little under 1/4 mile left again down another lane (signposted to Warkleigh). Look to your left for a superb view over the Taw and Mole valleys to a pretty patchwork of fields and woods. At the T-junction at Warkleigh turn left (signposted to Chittlehamholt). After 100 yards, just beyond the old school, you will see a gate on your right with a public footpath sign pointing to it.

Turn off here and follow a green lane for a short distance until it swings right into a field. Keep to the left-hand boundary of the field. At the end the hedge swings slightly right and you go through a gate onto a track; turn left. The track emerges onto a lane; cross it to a stile and keep to the left in the field beyond. Go through a gate at the end and keep to the left again. If you look to your left you get another lovely view across the rich farmland. Go through another gate onto a lane. *(1 1/2 miles)*

❹ Turn left and follow the lane for 300 yards until it swings right to a house. When it does, go straight on down a green lane, following the public footpath sign. It takes you down into a delightful little wood and across a stream. It then climbs quite steeply out of the valley and you get another good view ahead and to the right. Almost 3/4 mile after you joined it the green lane ends at a gate. Go through and cross a farmyard to a stile. Keep to the left of a field; the path runs between a hedge on the left and a gorse thicket on the right. Cross another stile into a wood.

Follow the path along the top of the wood, and when it joins a track bear right. After 250 yards or so this track joins another; bear left. The track swings to the right and joins yet another one; bear left again. You are now in the middle of Shortridge Wood, a large conifer plantation. The track swings left and you come to a gate. Go through that and two more gates, the last of which brings you onto the lane you followed on the outward leg. Turn right to return to the village and the pub. *(2 miles)*

Date walk completed:

....

Places of Interest Nearby

Six miles north-east of Chittlehamholt is South Molton, home of **Quince Honey Farm**, where you can see a working apiary. Telephone: 01769 572401. About 4 1/2 miles to the north-west is the **Cobbaton Combat Collection**, a comprehensive collection of militaria. Telephone: 01769 540740.

Rackenford 8 

The Stag Inn

This pretty country ramble takes you from the attractive village of Rackenford across farm fields and along delightful green lanes to the wastes of Witheridge Moor. Quiet lanes and more farm paths lead back to the village and the pub. There are some pleasant views across the rich mid-Devon countryside from some of the higher points, and a wealth of hedgerow flowers add colour to the route in summer.

Distance: *6 miles*

OS Explorer 114 Exeter and the Exe Valley
GR 851181

A fairly easy walk, mainly flat, but with some rough and muddy patches after rain

Starting point: The Stag Inn. You can leave your car in the car park while walking, but please ask first. Otherwise there is usually space in the road outside.

How to get there: Turn south off the A361 North Devon Link Road a few miles west of Tiverton and follow the signs for Rackenford. The pub is in the centre of the village.

The **Stag Inn**, built in the 12th century, claims to be the oldest hostelry in Devon. It is entered via a cobbled passageway, off which there is a very attractive bar, with a slate floor, a low ceiling, black beams and an open fireplace. Behind it are two delightful snug eating areas, one carpeted, the other with a stone floor. The whole place oozes atmosphere, and is said to be haunted by the ghost of Tom King, a notorious local highwayman. The food is all home-made from local produce, and ranges from ploughman's lunches to specials such as cottage pie, lasagne and roast beef.

Telephone: *01884 881369.*

The Walk

❶ Turn right as you leave the pub and then immediately right again along a narrow path alongside it. At the bottom turn right and then almost immediately left, following the public footpath sign. Go through a gate and keep to the right of a field. Cross a stile in the far right-hand corner and go straight across the next field to a gate, a footbridge and another gate. Go straight across the next field to another gate. Cross the next field about 20 yards in from the right-hand boundary and you will come to a track; walk along that to a gate into a farmyard. Go through the farmyard and follow the track round to the right and then to the left.

It climbs for a while, but 100 yards after the bend you will see a small gate on your right. Go through it and keep to the right of the field on the other side to another gate. Bear left on the other side,

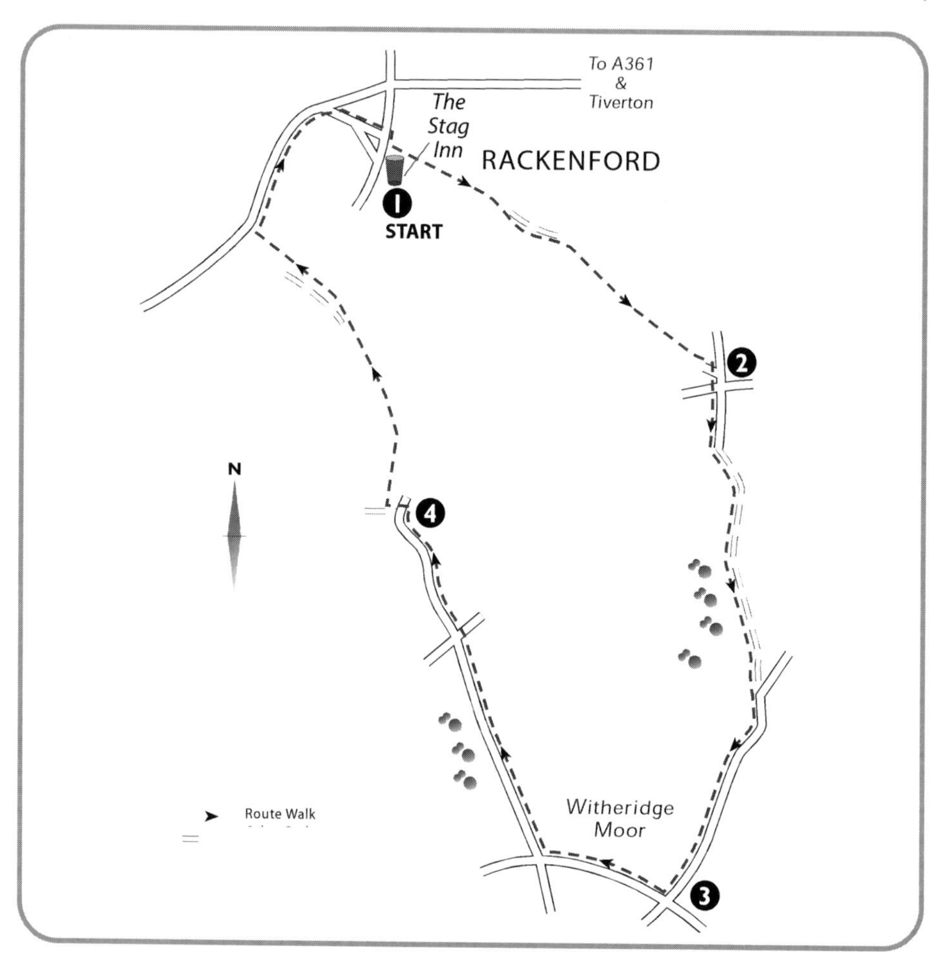

and you will enjoy a pleasant view of the farmland around you. Cross a stile and turn right and then left to cross another stile. Turn right and follow the right-hand boundary of the field beyond, with another typical Devon view to your left. In the far corner, cross a stile and then a footbridge. Cross the next field to a gate in the fence on the right. In the next field, aim for the gap between a house and a barn ahead of you. Go through a gate and out onto a lane. *(1¼ miles)*

❷ Turn right, and after 50 yards you will come to a crossroads; go straight across (signposted to Templeton). When this lane ends, go straight on along a green lane among some trees and cross a small stream. It climbs slightly and at the top there is a T-junction; go left, following the green lane. It is lovely along here, with the trees forming an arch above you. It can become muddy, however, so take care. You will find a wood on your right; look out for deer. After about ¾ mile you come out onto a lane; turn right. After a little over ½ mile you come to a crossroads. *(1½ miles)*

❸ Turn right (signposted to Rackenford). You pass the sedge- and gorse-covered Witheridge Moor, and at the next crossroads turn right again (signposted to Rackenford once more). After a while you come to another lovely avenue with the trees forming an arch overhead. At the next crossroads go straight on (still signposted to Rackenford). After 500 yards or so you will pass Hill Town. A short distance beyond it is the drive for West Hill Town; turn left along it. *(1½ miles)*

❹ As the drive turns left, cross a stile on your right. Bear left to another stile and turn right on the other side to follow the hedge on the right. You now get a lovely view to your left. Go through a gate at the end and keep to the right of the next field to another gate. Keep to the right again to reach two stiles. Bear slightly left across the next field to a footbridge and a gate. Go diagonally left on the other side, taking care as it can be quite boggy. Cross another footbridge and go half right to a gate. Bear left on the other side and you will be faced by two gates; go through the left-hand one into a broad green lane.

This stretch can also become rather muddy, but it is generally quite passable. After about 300 yards you go through a gate. Walk straight across the field beyond to another gate, leading into a lane; turn right. After 600 yards or so the lane swings right and you come to a junction; turn right and you will soon come to Rackenford. Pass the church and you will find the pub immediately in front of you at the end of the lane. *(1¾ miles)*

Date walk completed:

....

Places of Interest Nearby

Eight miles away is Tiverton, where you will find the **Grand Western Canal** and the historic **Tiverton Castle**. Telephone: 01884 255200. Just north of Tiverton is the 19th-century National Trust property of **Knightshayes Court**. Telephone: 01884 254665.

Walk 9 Kentisbeare

The Wyndham Arms

This delightful ramble combines quiet lanes with a pretty woodland stretch and some spectacular views. There is one fairly long hill in the middle, but it is steady rather than steep. Early summer is a good time to do it – that is when the hedgerow flowers are at their best, and the rhododendrons in the wood are magnificent.

Distance: *$5\frac{1}{2}$ miles*

OS Explorer 115 Exmouth and Sidmouth GR 068081

A relatively easy walk, with just one steady climb in the middle.

Starting point: The Wyndham Arms. The pub only has a forecourt for parking, so please do not leave your car there while walking. The best place to park is the village hall car park, signposted from the road as you enter the village.

How to get there: Turn north off the A373 Cullompton to Honiton road, following the signs for Kentisbeare.

The 14th-century building that is now the **Wyndham Arms** was originally the local manor, and the 16th-century fire plate bearing the arms of the Wyndham family can still be seen in the large fireplace in the main bar. The accommodation comprises two attractive bars, each with an enormous stone fireplace, a cosy little snug and a pretty courtyard at the back. A range of food is offered, from bar snacks to steaks, chicken and vegetarian options.

Telephone: *01884 266327.*

The Walk

❶ Turn right as you leave the pub and follow the road out of the village. When you come to the de-restriction sign, as the main road bends to the right and the road to Blackborough goes straight on, turn left along a footpath between hedges. Cross a stile, and shortly afterwards another one. Cross a track to a third stile and keep to the left of the field beyond. You get delightful views across the rolling farms and woods on either side and up ahead.

At the end of the field cross yet another stile and bear right across the next field. You will find some attractive fishing lakes on your left as you go down. Cross a fifth stile at the bottom, followed by a footbridge. The path on the other side brings you to one last stile and onto a lane. (½ mile)

❷ Turn left. Like most Devon lanes, you will find this one ablaze with flowers in the spring and summer. After a little under ½ mile you will come to a junction; walk round to the left, and after a few yards to the right, on the main lane, following the sign for Blackborough. The pretty view of the countryside on either side and the woodland on the hillside ahead remain with you on this stretch.

About ½ mile beyond the junction you pass a farm and the lane begins to climb steadily. It then swings to the right, and if you look right when the hedge ends you will get a magnificent view across the mid-Devon countryside. Near the top of the hill you come to the hamlet of Blackborough

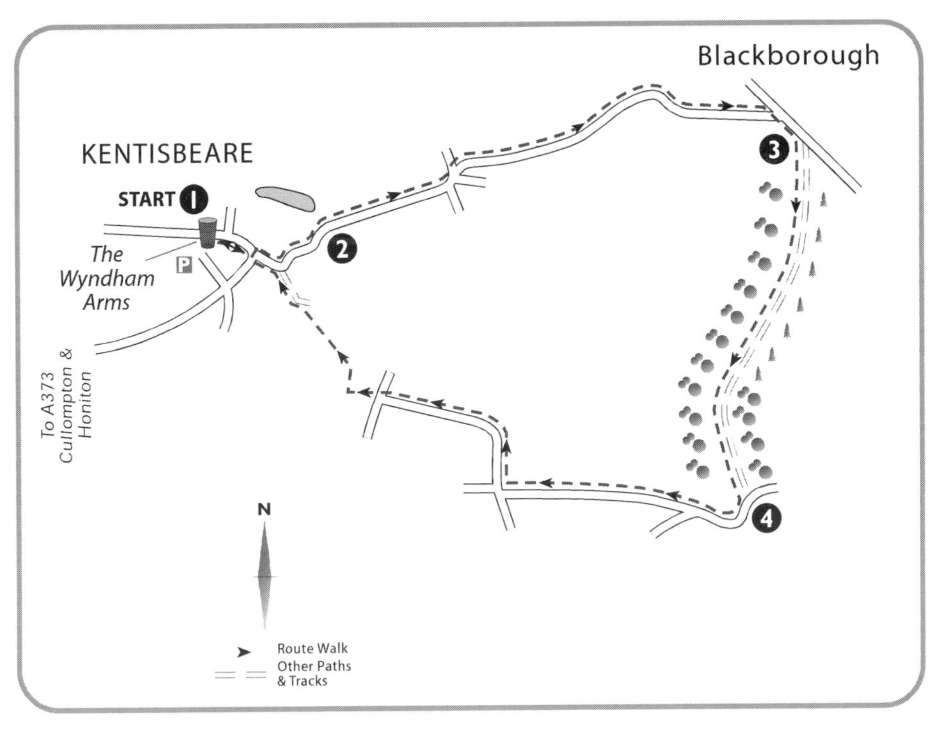

The lychgate, Kentisbeare church

and a T-junction; turn right. You continue to climb for a while and then enter a wood, where you will find a track on your right with a public bridlepath sign. Pause here and look to your right for another superb view across the country you have just walked through. *(1¾ miles)*

❸ Follow the track through the wood. This is a lovely stretch, with mixed woodland, mainly conifers on the left and broadleaved trees on the right, but it can become a bit muddy after rain. Ignore the smaller paths leading off the track, but where the main route forks bear right. Continue to ignore the smaller paths, keeping to the main track, which runs almost straight for some distance. A little over ½ mile after joining the track, the conifers that have dominated the wood on the left give way to rhododendrons, and then they take over on the right as well. You eventually come to a parking area, and get the best view yet to your right. *(1¼ miles)*

❹ Go through the parking area to a lane; turn right and follow it as it swings to the left and descends steeply. It then bends right. At the first junction go straight on, with the view across the valley now ahead of you. At the crossroads turn right (signposted to Orway). This lane soon swings left and passes a farm. At the T-junction at the end go straight on to a gate leading to a field. Keep to the left and at the end follow the field boundary round to the right to reach another gate.

Go half left across the next field to a stile in the far corner. Keep to the left of the next field and you will reach a gate and a track. Bear left and after a short distance you will come out at a lane; bear left again. After 200 yards you come to Kentisbeare; at the main road turn right, and you will find the pub on your left. *(2 miles)*

Date walk completed:

Places of Interest Nearby

About 4 miles north-west of Kentisbeare, near Willand, is the **Verbeer Manor Country Park.** **Telephone:** 01884 33212, and a similar distance to the north, near Uffculme, you will find **Cold Harbour Mill**, a working industrial museum. Telephone: 01884 840960.

The White Hart Hotel

This is a lovely and varied route that enables you to enjoy all the delights of this quiet area of mid-Devon: rich, rolling farmland, quiet lanes, beautiful views, pretty woodland – and the chance to visit a vineyard along the way. It heads south and then east along farm paths and little lanes, before joining the Two Moors Way, which takes you north towards Down St Mary. From there woodland and farm paths and an often flower-filled lane lead you back to Bow.

Distance: *7½ miles*

OS Explorer 113 Okehampton
GR 719018

A longish but easy walk, with just two not very steep climbs in the middle

Starting point: The White Hart Hotel. There is limited space in the pub car park and customers may leave their cars there while they walk (provided they ask first). Otherwise there is parking on the roads in the village.

How to get there: Bow is on the A3072 Crediton to Okehampton road.

The **White Hart Hotel** is a small, cosy 15th-century establishment, now no longer a hotel. The bar is half-timbered, with an enormous stone fireplace and a stone floor. Beyond it is the carpeted dining area, and there is also a games room with pool, darts and a television. At the back you will find a garden and children's play area, with a pretty pond. Good traditional pub fare is served here, ranging from jacket potatoes and burgers to main meals such as steak and ale pie, lasagne and Cajun chicken. Note, however, that they are not open at midday on Mondays.

Telephone: *01636 82966.*

The Walk

❶ Turn left from the pub, and after about 300 yards or so, turn right up Station Road (signposted to the village hall, Bow church and Spreyton). Leave the village, and as the lane turns sharp right, turn left along a concrete track. At the end, bear left into a field and keep to the right. Go through a gate into another field and walk to a stile. Cross the next field to meet a hedge and follow it, keeping it on your left. After 50 yards or so cross a stile on your left and keep to the right of the field on the other side. In the far right-hand corner cross another stile on your right. Keep to the left of a field to yet another stile, leading into a lane. Turn left and after 100 yards you will come to a T-junction. *(1¼ miles)*

❷ Turn right. At the junction after 700 yards go straight on (signposted to Coleford and Colebrooke). After another 600 yards you will see a sign for the Two Moors Way pointing sharp left. Turn through a gate and up a track for a few yards, then up some steps into a field on the right. At the top go right and immediately left around the edge of the field. At the end go right across a stile and then across a small footbridge and

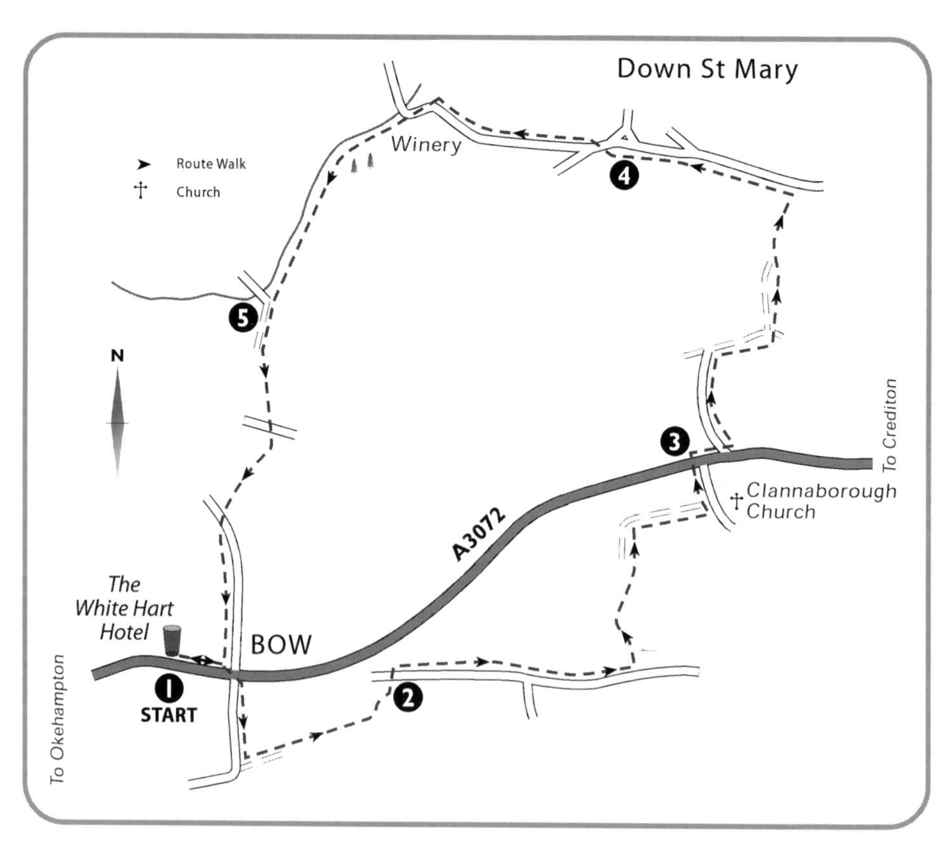

straight on into a field. Turn left along the hedge and after about 50 yards you will find a post with a Two Moors Way waymark pointing right across the field.

Cross the field to a gap in the hedge and follow the track on the other side. At the end follow the track round to the right, as indicated by the Two Moors Way sign. Keep on the track until it comes out onto a lane opposite the church at Clannaborough. Follow the lane for 200 yards to its junction with the main road. *(1 3/4 miles)*

❸ Turn right, and, after 150 yards, left up a lane, as indicated by the Two Moors Way sign. At the T-junction turn right along a track, still following the sign for the Two Moors Way. After 300 yards you will see a gate on your left marked with the waymark. Go through and follow a track along the edge of a field. At the end it goes right, then left, then right again. At the end go left through a gate onto a path through some trees. Cross a stile into a field and keep to the right until you come to another stile on your right; cross it into a wood.

Cross the footbridge on your left and and turn right across a field. Go through two gates, the second of which leads into a lane; turn left. The lane climbs towards Down St Mary. On the edge of the village it forks; go straight on along the main lane. *(1 1/2 miles)*

❹ At the next two junctions keep to the main lane again, and go right at the next fork (signposted to Zeal Monachorum and the vineyard). After a little over 1/2 mile you will come to the Down St Mary Vineyard, and the lane swings right across a bridge. Turn left through a gate immediately beyond the winery. Cross a field to another gate and then a third. Keep to the right of a field to a stile and keep to the right again to another stile. At the end of the conifer plantation, go through a gate into a field and keep to the right to a footbridge and another gate. Keep to the right of the next field to a gate leading into more trees. Go round a gate at the end onto a lane, with the attractive Tuckingmill Bridge on the right. *(1 1/2 miles)*

❺ Go straight on, and when you come to a gate leading to a house, go left, following the yellow waymark. Continue round to the left for a few yards to a gate on the right, where a yellow waymark points left. Do not follow it, but go through the gate and follow a track to another gate. Go straight on to a third gate, following the direction of the blue waymark, and keep to the left of a field to a gateway. Keep to the left again. One more gate takes you onto a lane. Cross to another gate, and bear slightly left across a field to yet another gate. Bear right across the next field until you meet a hedge; bear left and follow the hedge down to a gate. Cross the farmyard and follow a drive to a lane. Turn right, and at the T-junction, left. At the T-junction in Bow, where the lane meets the main road, turn right to return to the pub. *(1 1/2 miles)*

Date walk completed:

....

Places of Interest Nearby

Down St Mary Vineyard. Telephone: 01363 82300. At Okehampton, 10 miles away, are the ruins of **Okehampton Castle** (English Heritage). Telephone: 01837 52844.

Walk 11 Colyton

The Kingfisher

Colyton is a delightful little town, with narrow streets and lanes of stone houses and cottages, and is worth exploring in its own right. The area to the north is criss-crossed by green lanes, which are tranquil havens for flowers and wildlife. This route explores some of these old byways, as well as farm paths and quiet surfaced lanes. For most of the walk you are in the depths of the countryside, where the silence is broken only by the song of the birds. There are some lovely riverside stretches and superb views.

Distance: *7 miles*

OS Explorer 116 Lyme Regis and Bridport GR 246940

A moderate walk, but with some steady climbs and a few muddy and wet stretches

Starting point: The public car park (pay & display) in Dolphin Street, Colyton. The Kingfisher has no parking.

How to get there: Turn north off the A3052 between Sidmouth and Lyme Regis, either just before Colyford (if approaching from the Sidmouth direction) or in Colyford itself (coming from Lyme Regis). Follow the signs to the town centre. Dolphin Street runs off the central square.

The **Kingfisher** is a comfortable, welcoming pub near the centre of Colyton, dating back to the 17th century. The bar has exposed half-timbered stone walls and low beams, and although it is quite large, it has a snug feel. It is carpeted and has a big open fireplace. Behind it is a light, airy family room, which leads into a pretty beer garden with an arbour. Traditional pub food is served, as well as such delicacies as barbecued spare ribs. The snack menu ranges from jacket potatoes to salads and sandwiches – the prawn sandwiches are particularly popular.

Telephone: *01297 552476.*

The Walk

❶ Cross Dolphin Street to a small street to the right of the Colcombe Castle Hotel. Follow this on the other side as it winds past the church to a T-junction; turn right into King Street, and leave Colyton. Cross the River Coly and at the fork in the lane about 200 yards further on, go right (signposted to Umborne). Just beyond the farm on the right, at a public footpath sign that appears to be pointing straight along the road, turn right and cross a stile. Bear left in the field beyond.

Last time I walked this route there was a stile halfway across without a fence on either side. Pass it and continue to the far corner; cross a stile and keep to the right of another field to another stile. Keep to the right of the next field and halfway along cross the stile on your right and turn left to follow a path alongside the stream. Soon it swings right to cross a footbridge; bear left across a field on the other side to a stile. Cut diagonally left across another field to another footbridge. Keep to the right on the other side along a long field, with the stream again on your right.

At the end cross a stile and continue alongside the stream until you come to another footbridge; cross it and bear left on the other side to yet another

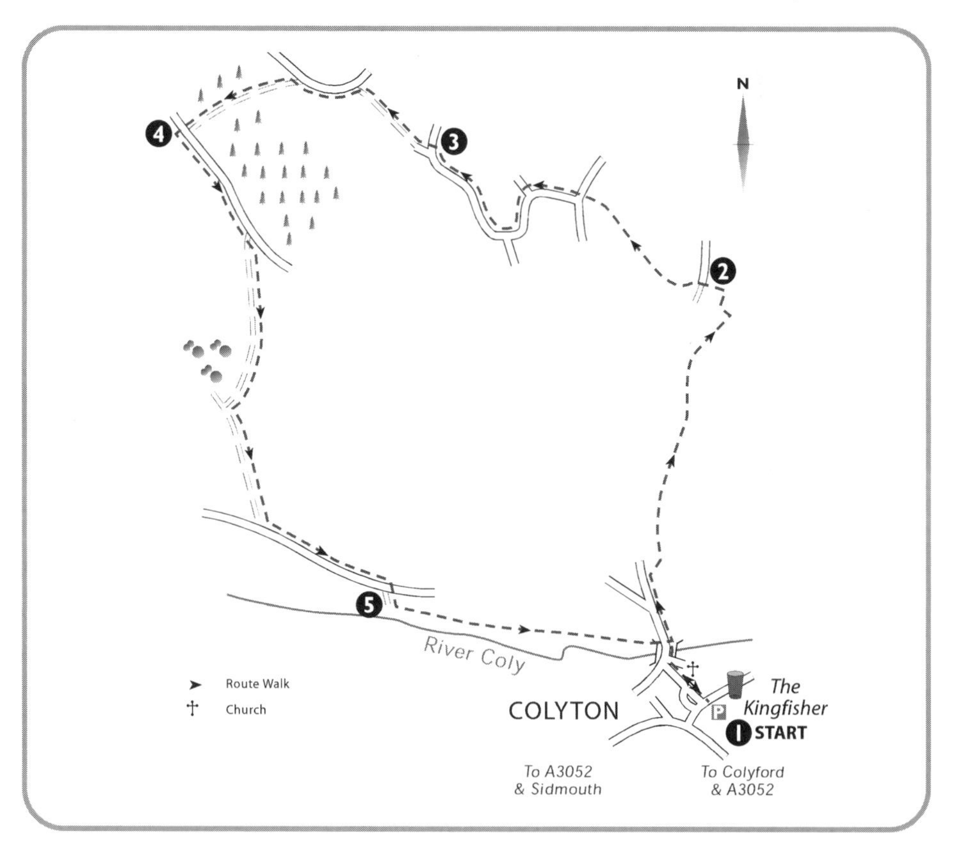

footbridge. Go over the next field to a gap in the hedge leading onto a track; cross it to a stile and turn left in the field beyond. Follow the fence round and cross a footbridge and stile on your left and make for the stile in the middle of the next fence. Cross the next field to a kissing-gate leading onto a drive. *(1¾ miles)*

❷ Cross to a path that runs to the left of a house. Go over a footbridge and then a stile. Keep to the right across a field and cross a footbridge at the end. Turn right on the other side and you will come to a kissing-gate on your right; go through that and another kissing-gate immediately beyond it. Cut across the next field, keeping to the right, and cross two stiles separated by a footbridge. Cross another field to a kissing-gate; bear left on the other side and you will find a stile alongside the stream, leading onto a lane.

Turn left and then right (signposted to Umborne). At the junction 300 yards further on follow the main lane round to the left. At the next junction go right. The lane now climbs steadily. At the next junction, after about 600 yards, as the main lane bends to the right, go straight on up another lane. *(1¼ miles)*

❸ At the end of this lane, bear right along a green lane which continues to climb steadily. You emerge onto a lane; bear left and continue to climb. After ¼ mile take a green lane going off to the left. After a while it enters a pretty wood and finally emerges onto a lane. *(1 mile)*

❹ Turn left, and after 600 yards you will see yet another green lane on the right. Follow it as it begins to descend into the valley of the Coly. After a few hundred yards you go through a gate and continue descending. You pass a wood on the right. Just beyond it you join another green lane; bear left.

After 700 yards or so go through a gate into a farmyard. Turn right and follow the farm drive to a lane; turn left. At the junction, go straight on (signposted to Colyton). Half a mile after you joined the lane you will see a track on the right leading towards a large footbridge. Turn down it and bear left before the bridge. *(2 miles)*

❺ You are now on the East Devon Way. Cross a small footbridge and a stile. Keep to the right, alongside the river, then cut across to a kissing-gate followed by a footbridge. Cross the next field to another footbridge followed by another kissing-gate. A wood and two fields follow, separated by kissing gates.

About 150 yards into the second field you go through a kissing-gate on the right and follow the path alongside the river for a while then go back into the field. Keep to the riverbank and go through one last kissing-gate onto the lane you came out on. Turn right, cross the river and take the first left. At the square, go to the left of the hotel to the car park. The Kingfisher is down to the left. *(1 mile)*

Date walk completed:

....

Places of Interest Nearby

There are **tram rides** between Colyton and Seaton. About 2 miles north of Colyton is **Shute Barton**, a medieval manor house owned by the National Trust. Telephone: 01297 34692.

South Tawton 12 Walk

The Seven Stars Inn

Variety is the hallmark of this lovely route, which starts with pretty lanes and farm tracks that lead to the edge of Dartmoor, from where you get the most stunning views across the farms and woods to the north. You then skirt the moor edge, enjoying the stillness and the views, for almost 2 miles before joining the infant River Taw, the setting for Henry Williamson's classic *Tarka the Otter*. You have the opportunity to visit a working water-powered forge in Sticklepath before returning to South Tawton along a green lane. There is a steady climb to the moor, and once there the route might be a bit tricky in poor visibility, but there is little rough terrain and in good visibility you are unlikely to go wrong.

***Distance:** 5¼ miles*

OS Explorer OL28 Dartmoor
GR 653943

A fairly challenging walk, with some steady climbing towards the start; the going, however, is quite easy

Starting point: The Seven Stars Inn. There is no pub car park, but you should be able to find space to park in the village centre.

How to get there: The village lies just south of the A30 Exeter to Okehampton road. From Exeter, leave the A30 at Whiddon Down. From the Okehampton direction, leave it just east of Okehampton. In both cases you should then follow the signs to South Zeal and then to South Tawton.

This 19th-century creeper-clad, stone-built **Seven Stars Inn** is strategically placed in the centre of South Tawton, just by the church. It comprises a cosy, panelled bar with little alcoves off it to one side of the entrance and a light, airy family room on the other. Both have enormous stone fireplaces containing wood-burning stoves and there are stone pillars and exposed beams throughout. The menu is extensive and ranges from soup and snacks such as crab cakes and jacket potatoes to steaks and chicken dishes. There is also an impressive array of whiskies and wines.

Telephone: *01837 840292.*

The Walk

❶ Turn left as you leave the pub and follow the lane out of the village. As you go you get a good view ahead to Dartmoor. At the junction after about 300 yards, turn left (signposted to Dishcombe). At the next junction go straight on. You descend to cross a small stream. Shortly afterwards, turn right at a crossroads (signposted to South Zeal). This lane climbs to a T-junction on the edge of South Zeal. Turn left and continue to climb. After 50 yards turn right up another lane, still climbing. *(3/4 mile)*

❷ You come out at another T-junction. Turn right and then immediately left up a lane. After 100 yards, as the lane swings left, turn off to the right. There is no signpost, but it is a clear path through the bracken. At the fork go left and at the next fork left again. You cross another broad, green path and after a while your path begins to descend fairly steeply. At the bottom the path swings to the left and comes out at a lane.

Bear left and after 50 yards turn right along a track between walls. It is signposted to the moor, but the sign is hidden from this side by a wall. There is a short muddy stretch and then you cross a stream. The track begins to climb, and becomes fairly rocky as it does so. At the junction bear left and at the next one go straight on, still climbing. After another

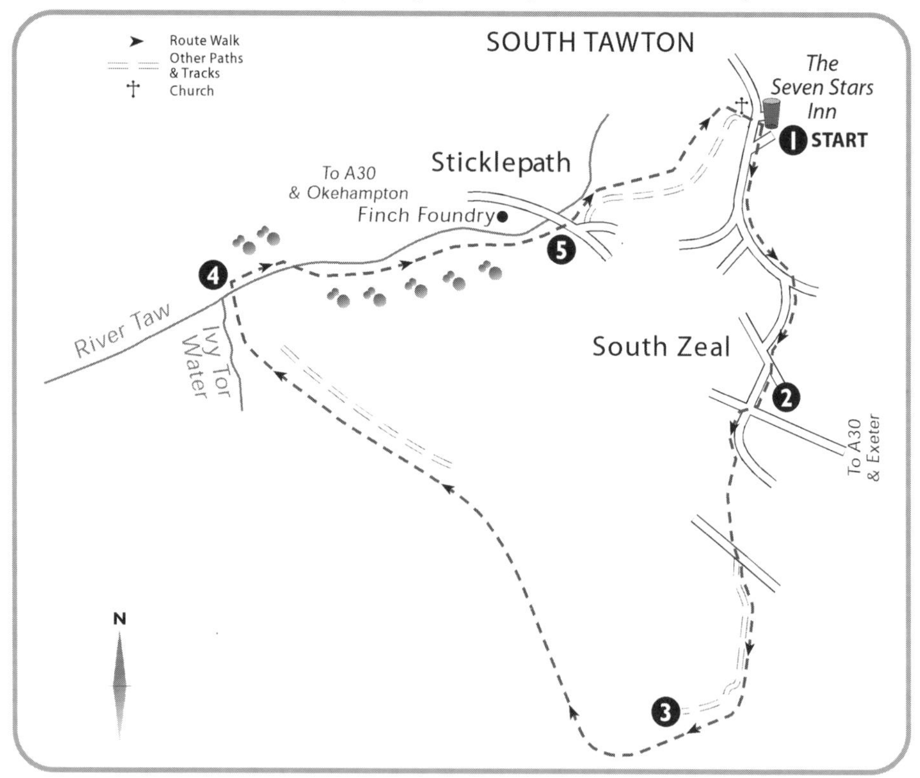

300 yards or so you come to a gate leading onto the open moor. *(1 mile)*

3 After enjoying the stunning view behind you, follow the wall on your right and when it bears to the right go straight on. You will soon meet another wall on your right; follow that until it too swings right, and then follow it round. You should now keep parallel to the wall; there is no need to follow it precisely as it winds in and out, but it is a good idea to keep it in sight. There is a path through the bracken about 200 yards or so uphill from it, but if you can't find it, just make your own way – as long as you can see the wall and are not climbing the slope on your left, you will be fine.

If you are following the main path you will find that it meets the wall after about ¾ mile. When the wall goes right, don't follow it round, but bear left through the bracken to meet up with another clear path; bear right. You cross a small stream and come to some rather dilapidated walls. Cross them, keeping the main wall on your right, and on the other side you will find a track. Follow that, and where it forks, go straight on alongside the wall. When that turns right go straight on along the track. After about ¼ mile you will come to another wall. When that also swings right, keep to the track, which goes straight on. It eventually becomes a path and meets a stream. Follow the path down alongside the stream and you will come out at the River Taw by a footbridge. *(1¾ miles)*

4 Cross over and climb to a path on the other side; turn right. You are now on the Tarka Trail, a long-distance route that takes in the various places in which Henry Williamson's *Tarka the Otter* is set. After 200 yards you will see a path going right, down to the river (signposted to Sticklepath). Follow it to a footbridge carved with quotations from *Tarka the Otter*. On this bank the path is lined with rhododendrons, which make a magnificent display in early summer. Cross a stile and continue alongside the river until you meet a track. Turn left and go through a gate. After a short distance cross the footbridge on the left if you want to visit Finch Foundry, a 19th-century water-powered forge, now owned by the National Trust and still operating. If you do so, then leave via the main entrance and turn right along the road to rejoin the walk. Otherwise continue along the track and you will come out at a road. *(1 mile)*

5 Cross over to a lane marked with a cycle route sign. After 50 yards turn left up a green lane (marked as the route of the Tarka Trail). It climbs quite steeply initially and then levels off somewhat. After a while it begins to descend and meets a surfaced lane at the edge of South Tawton. Go down to the village centre and you will find the pub ahead of you. *(¾ mile)*

Date walk completed:

....

Places of Interest Nearby

About 4 miles away is Okehampton, which is home to the **Museum of Dartmoor Life.** Telephone: 01837 52295. Also worth a visit are the impressive ruins of **Okehampton Castle** (English Heritage). Telephone: 01837 52844.

Walk **13 Cheriton Bishop**

The Old Thatch Inn

This is a lovely walk at any time, but it is at its very best in spring, when the woods and surrounding slopes are carpeted with bluebells. We take quiet lanes and green lanes down to the beautiful valley of the River Teign, and then follow the river through a mixture of conifers and broadleaved woods before returning to Cheriton Bishop along farm tracks and woodland paths.

***Distance:** 8 miles*

OS Explorer OL28 Dartmoor
GR 774930

A moderate walk along lanes and easy paths, with just one stiff climb about two-thirds of the way round

Starting point: The Old Thatch Inn. The pub car park can become rather crowded, so the landlord would prefer walkers not to leave their cars there. There is plenty of parking in the road, however.

How to get there: The village is about ½ mile south of the A30 Exeter to Okehampton road. From Exeter, leave at the Woodleigh junction about 10 miles from Exeter. From the Okehampton direction, leave at Whiddon Down and follow the old A30 for 5 miles. The village is clearly signposted from both directions.

The 17th-century **Old Thatch Inn**, once a coaching house, later served as a tearoom and restaurant, and was only licensed again in 1974. It is a lovely building with low beamed ceilings and divided into two cosy rooms by a magnificent granite fireplace. The menu is mouthwatering, ranging from the usual bar snacks, such as sandwiches and ploughman's lunches, to delicious steaks and fish dishes, as well as a popular cottage pie. Duck is a particular speciality. Another feature is the beer festival, held every year over the spring bank holiday weekend.

Telephone: 01647 24204.

The Walk

❶ Turn right from the pub and then almost immediately right again (signposted to Dunsford and Clifford Bridge). As you follow this pretty lane, look to the right for a good view across to Dartmoor, a view that stays with you on and off for most of this stretch. After 1¼ miles you come to a junction; turn right (signposted to East Down and West Down).

After another ¼ mile, when the lane ends at East Down, go straight on along a green lane (signposted to the road near Scotley Bridge). After 250 yards or so you will come to a junction with another green lane; go straight on. Towards the end you enter a small wood and, about ½ mile after joining the green lane, you go through a gate and down to a lane. *(2 miles)*

❷ Bear left. As you follow this lane you will see the River Teign below you through the trees on your right. The lane descends, swings to the right and climbs again. After 500 yards turn right at a crossroads (signposted to Clifford Bridge and Moretonhampstead). Go down and cross

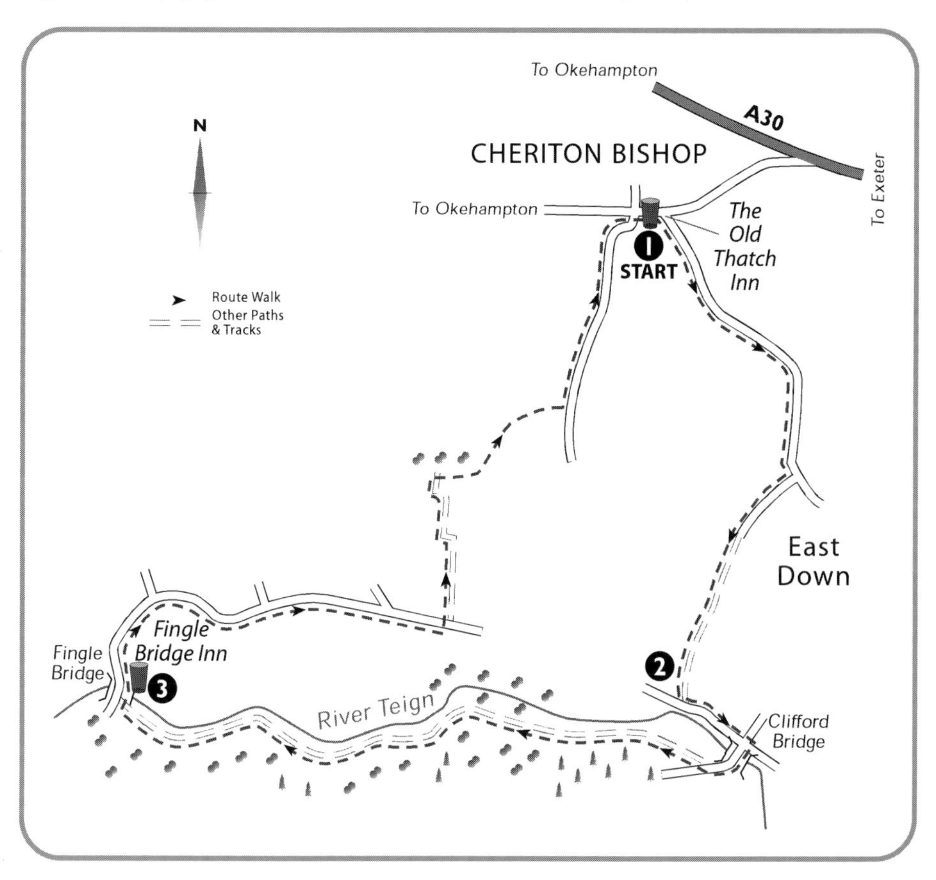

Fingle Bridge

Clifford Bridge. On the other side you climb slightly, and just beyond some houses you will find a gate and stile on the right leading into a conifer plantation, with a signposted pointing to Fingle Bridge. Cross the stile and follow the broad track through the trees on the other side.

The track soon meets up with the river and meanders alongside it. After a while the conifers give way to broadleaved trees. From time to time the track leaves the river and then rejoins it, and the broadleaves alternate with conifers. After 2¼ miles of delightful woodland walking you go through a gate and come to a car park and picnic area. Cross it and turn right across Fingle Bridge at the end. If you are ready for refreshment, you will find the Fingle Bridge Inn on the riverbank on your right. *(2¾ miles)*

❸ Carry straight on along the lane on the other side of the bridge. After 500 yards turn right at the junction. The lane climbs steeply for ¼ mile or so and then levels off. Look to the left as you follow it for a typical Devon scene. You pass two lanes on the left leading to Crockernwell; carry straight on and about 300 yards beyond the second one turn left along a track (signposted as a public footpath to Coombe Hall). Cross a cattle grid and follow the track to a barn; when you reach it, follow the track to the left and right again.

Go left at some farm buildings and at the T-junction turn right. Go through a gate and follow the path on the other side to another gate. Cross a stream and turn right. Follow the path alongside a fence. Go through a gate and across a small footbridge, and turn left. After a few yards, there is a path junction; go straight on (signposted to Lower Eggbeer). You climb gently through the trees and emerge onto a gorse-covered hillside. Pause on your way up and admire the rolling countryside all around you. Go through a gate at the top and keep to the left of the field beyond. At the end go right and after 50 yards left through a gate. Keep to the right of the next field to reach a gate leading onto a lane. Turn left and follow the lane, looking back from time to time for a last expansive view across the countryside to Dartmoor. After ¾ mile you will find yourself back in Cheriton Bishop; turn right at the main road to return to the pub. *(3¼ miles)*

Date walk completed:

....

Places of Interest Nearby

About 4 miles south-west of Cheriton Bishop is the National Trust property of **Castle Drogo**, a country house designed by Sir Edwin Lutyens and built in the early part of the 20th century. Telephone; 01647 433306. Ten miles to the east is **Exeter**, with its cathedral, city walls, museums and other attractions.

Knowle 14 Walk

The Dog & Donkey

This is a walk for flower-lovers. It takes in Lympstone and East Budleigh Commons, part of the East Devon Pebblebed Heath Site of Special Scientific Interest, which is carpeted with gorse and heather in late summer. It also includes lanes, green lanes and paths that are filled with a mass of other flowers in season. And there is an added bonus in the form of lovely views from the higher ground.

Distance: *4½ miles*

OS Explorer 115 Exmouth and Sidmouth GR 051826

An easy walk along clear lanes and paths, with virtually no hills

Starting point: The Dog & Donkey. You should be able to park in the road, or else at the village hall nearby.

How to get there: Knowle is on the northern outskirts of Budleigh Salterton, and can be reached via the B3180 or B3178 from the A3052 Exeter to Sidmouth road, or via the B3179 from the A376 between Exeter and Exmouth. Follow the signs for Budleigh Salterton and just before you reach the town, look for the sign to Knowle. The pub is on the main road through the village.

The **Dog & Donkey** is a relatively new establishment, having been built in 1926 – although the previous pub on this site had this name, how it originated is a mystery. The welcoming main bar has a tiled floor and a wood-burning stove, and the walls are decorated with old photographs. There is also a function room and a pretty beer garden. A good variety of home-cooked food is offered, ranging from sandwiches to steaks and a range of curries, as well as daily specials.

Telephone: *01395 442021.*

The Walk

1 Turn right and after a few yards left along a lane. Continue past the interesting little St John's church, with its pretty garden, quite unlike the usual churchyard. After about ½ mile, as the lane swings left, go straight on towards Dalditch Farm. As the main track goes right to the farm, go straight on along a green lane, following the public footpath and public bridlepath signs. This is a very pretty stretch, with hedgerows on either side that are flower-filled in season.

After 300 yards, you will see a public footpath sign pointing half left. Leave the green lane and follow the path through some trees to emerge onto a stretch of heathland covered in heather and western gorse – a mass of yellow and pink in late summer. The path continues through a belt of trees to another piece of open ground. Turn right to follow the edge to the attractive Squabmoor Reservoir. Keep to the right of the reservoir, and at the end you come out onto another piece of gorse- and heather-covered heathland. Where the path forks, go right, through

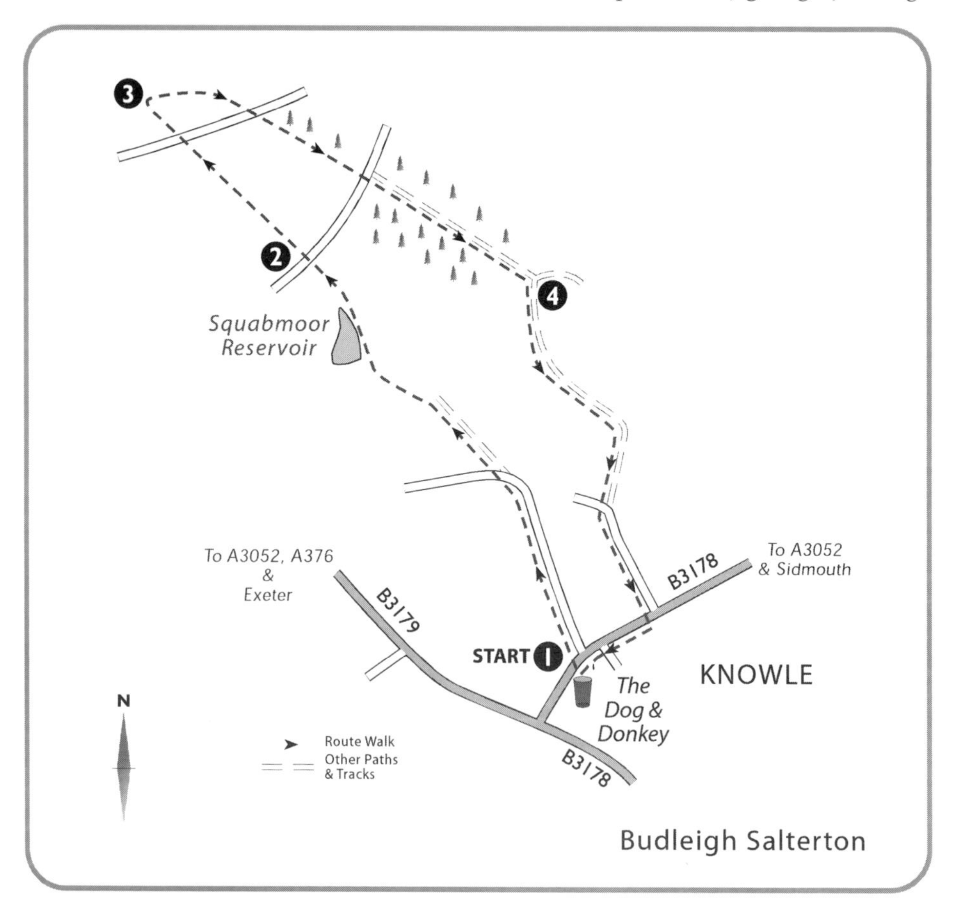

some trees to a parking area and a lane. *(1¼ miles)*

❷ Cross the lane to another path; where it forks on the other side, keep right to reach another area of heathland. Here you will find orchids, tormentil and the delicate milkwort dotted among the usual gorse and heather in summer. You cross a track and then come to a small stretch of woodland. About 750 yards after crossing the lane, you come to another road. Go left and then immediately right onto more heathland. After another 150 yards or so you will come to a clear, broad path crossing the one you are on. Turn right along it. *(½ mile)*

Squabmoor reservoir

❸ You are now on the East Devon Way, which takes you into a wood and then out into a clearer area with common gorse, taller than the western gorse of the heath and earlier-flowering, alongside you. After about 600 yards you come out at a road; turn left and then right, following the public footpath sign. You continue among the trees and gorse, and soon you will get a lovely view down towards the coast on your right.

After another 600 yards you come out onto a lane. Cross it and go over the car park on the other side to a track that takes you into a plantation. Follow the track straight down through the trees. When it bends to the left, follow it and then turn right down another track, marked with a yellow public footpath waymark. Follow this track down until it joins a green lane. *(1¼ miles)*

❹ Bear right and follow this lovely green lane, ignoring paths and tracks on either side, until, after about ¾ mile, you emerge onto a surfaced lane. Bear left and follow this lane as it crosses the old Budleigh Salterton to Exmouth railway and finally comes out onto the main road. Turn right, and after ¼ mile you will find the Dog & Donkey on your left. *(1½ miles)*

Date walk completed:

....

Places of Interest Nearby

Just beyond East Budleigh, 2½ miles north-east of Knowle, is **Bicton Park**, over 60 acres of botanical gardens. Telephone: 01395 568465. About 3 miles to the west, on the outskirts of Exmouth, is the National Trust property of **A La Ronde**, a unique 16-sided house built in the 18th century. Telephone: 01395 265514.

Walk 15 Postbridge

The East Dart Hotel

This is a lovely moorland amble, which gives you a sense of the enormous skies and wide open spaces of Dartmoor without very much effort. There are wild flowers to enjoy along the way in season, and a cool conifer plantation, but the main attraction is likely to be the superb views over the moors and tors.

Distance: *5¾ miles*

OS Explorer OL28 Dartmoor
GR 649789 (pub), 646788 (car park)

A relatively easy walk, with just a couple of climbs in the middle

Starting point: The public car park at Postbridge (free, donations invited). The pub has only limited parking.

How to get there: Postbridge is on the B3212 between Moretonhampstead and Princetown, and both the pub and the car park are on that road.

The **East Dart Hotel** is a favourite watering hole for walkers. The main bar has a wooden floor, low beams and a wood-burning stove. There is also a small, attractive carpeted eating area and a garden and patio at the back. The food, which is all home cooked and locally sourced where possible, ranges from rolls and soups to steak and ale pie, smoked trout and chicken and mushroom pie. Scrumptious Devon cream teas are also available.

Telephone: 01822 880213.

The Walk

❶ Turn left as you leave the car park and cross the bridge over the East Dart River. As you do so, notice the medieval clapper bridge on your right. On the other side you will see a drive on the right, which leads to Lydgate House Hotel and is also signposted as a public bridlepath. The East Dart Hotel is just beyond it.

Turn along the drive and at the entrance to Lydgate House go through the gate. Take the path that goes to the right of the hotel to another gate. Keep to the left of the field beyond. Go through a gap in the wall towards the end, and continue with the wall now on your right. The path meanders through the gorse, which is most attractive in early summer. Go through a gate and continue along the clear path on the other side to another gate. The path bends to the left. At the end of the field, when you reach another gate, do not go through it but swing right to follow the wall. Here you have the first of a succession of good views across the moor to your right. Go through a small gate at the end and follow the path on the other side. *(3/4 mile)*

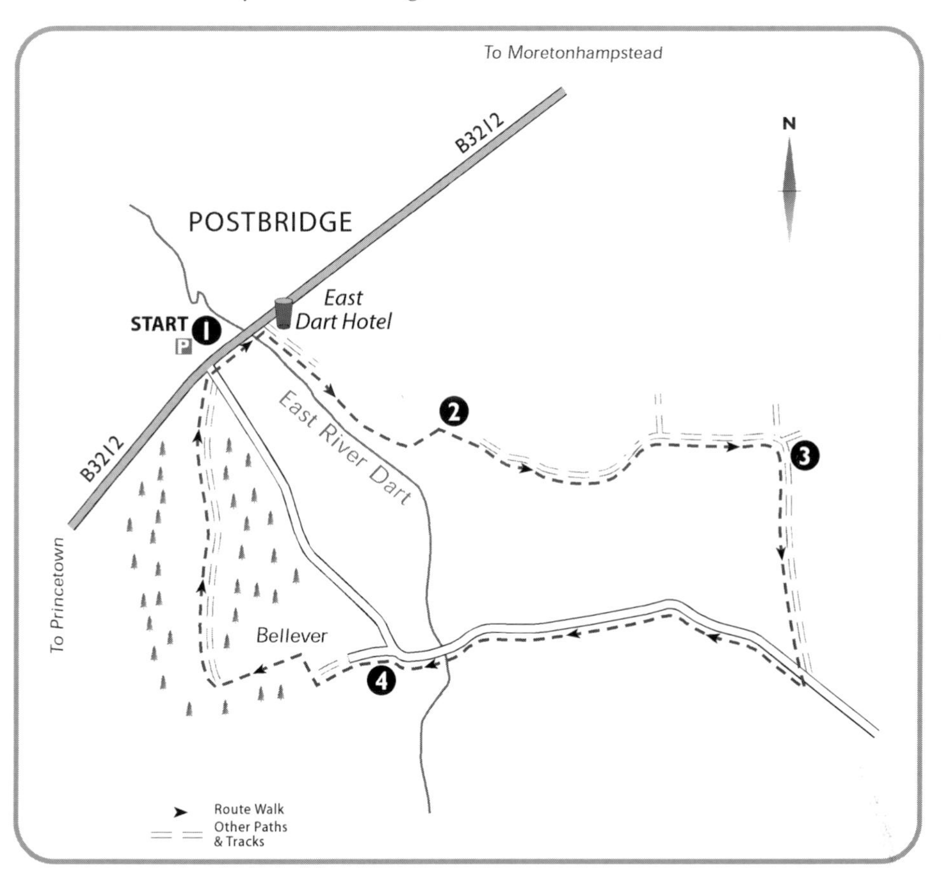

The ancient stone bridge at Bellever

❷ You join a track, which soon swings right; follow it round to a gate. On the other side there is usually a stream running along the track for a short distance, so you might prefer to keep to the grass alongside it. You finally come to a T-junction; turn left (signposted to Pizwell). Go through a gate. The track goes left past a house, through another gate and swings right past a few more buildings.

When it emerges on the other side and swings left, go straight on along a less clear track. You cross a small stream via stepping stones, with another good moorland view over to your right. You are now surrounded by heather and gorse. About 600 yards beyond the buildings you will come to a crossroads. *(1¼ miles)*

❸ Turn right through a gate. You soon pass a gate set incongruously on its own in the middle of the open moor, with no fence or wall on either side. Where the track forks, go right to another solitary gate. Pass it, following the path sign, and look to your right for a superb view across northern Dartmoor. You finally come to a gate that is set in a fence; turn right in the lane beyond.

This lane takes you through some typical moorland scenery. It swings to the left and begins to climb, steadily but not too steeply. When you reach the crest of the rise you get a good view across to the right, with Bellever Forest ahead of you and Bellever Tor beyond. A mile after joining the lane you cross the East Dart River again and then, a little further on, pass the entrance to the forest. *(2¼ miles)*

❹ A hundred yards beyond the forest entrance, as the main lane swings right, go straight on past the youth hostel. When the surfaced lane ends, go straight on along a grassy track, which climbs to a gate. The track continues to climb on the other side to another gate, leading into the plantation. On the other side turn right to skirt the plantation for a while. The path then swings left among the trees and crosses a track. Continue along it, but at the next track turn right. If you look right along this stretch you get the best view of all. Ignore the side tracks to the right and left and continue along the main route to a gate. Follow the track round to the right to a road; turn left and cross a cattle grid to another road. Turn right here and the car park is on your left. *(1½ miles)*

Date walk completed:

....

Places of Interest Nearby
The **Powder Mills Pottery**, which is open to the public at certain times, is 1¼ miles south-west of Postbridge. Telephone: 01822 880263. Four miles further on is Princetown, where you will find the **High Moorland Visitor Centre**. Telephone: 01822 890414.

Stokeinteignhead

The Church House Inn

This is a walk of quite stunning views. Starting from the delightful village of Stokeinteignhead (pronounced 'Stoke-in-teen-head'), with its thatched cottages and little lanes, we follow a green lane down to the equally pretty village of Maidencombe on the coast, where we join the South West Coast Path for a strenuous but beautiful stretch around Babbacombe Bay. The route back to Stokeinteignhead follows more green lanes. In addition to the miles of coast to be seen from the Coast Path, there are lovely views across the undulating farmland and up the valley of the River Teign to Dartmoor.

Distance: *6 miles*

OS Explorer 110 Torquay and Dawlish GR 916705

A challenging walk, with some steep hills along the coast; the green lanes in particular can become wet after rain, so do go suitably shod

Starting point: The Church House Inn. Patrons can leave their cars in the car park (with permission) while walking. Alternatively, park along the lanes in the village, being sure not to block entrances or restrict the carriageway.

How to get there: The village is signposted off the A379 Torquay to Shaldon road at various points. If you are approaching from the Newton Abbot side, take the road to Shaldon and turn off at Combeinteignhead, following the signs to Stokeinteignhead.

The **Church House Inn** is a delightful cob and thatch hostelry that dates back to the 13th century and has the heavy beams one associates with that era. It comprises a snug little bar and a spacious lounge with a dining area leading off it, all very tastefully furnished and carpeted. Much of the furniture is antique, and there is an inglenook fireplace. Outside there is a pretty beer garden. The food is all home-made, and ranges from salads, sandwiches and ploughman's lunches to rib eye steaks, steak and kidney pie and a variety of fish and vegetarian dishes.

Telephone: 01626 872475.

The Walk

❶ Turn left from the pub and follow the lane as it climbs out of the village. At the top of the hill you will see a lane on the left; follow it and after a few yards turn left up a green lane between two houses called Two Hoots and Oaklands. This also climbs, and as it does so you get a good view to the left over Stokeinteignhead. When the green lane forks, follow the right-hand branch. It can become rather wet underfoot after rain, especially towards the top, so take care.

At the top, as the hedges open out you will come to a junction, with a path going right; go straight on. At the next junction, with a path going left, go straight on again. About 300 yards after this second junction, you join a lane. *(1 mile)*

❷ Go straight on along the lane. After about ¼ mile it curves left and starts to descend, and you get a lovely view across to Babbacombe Bay. You soon reach the

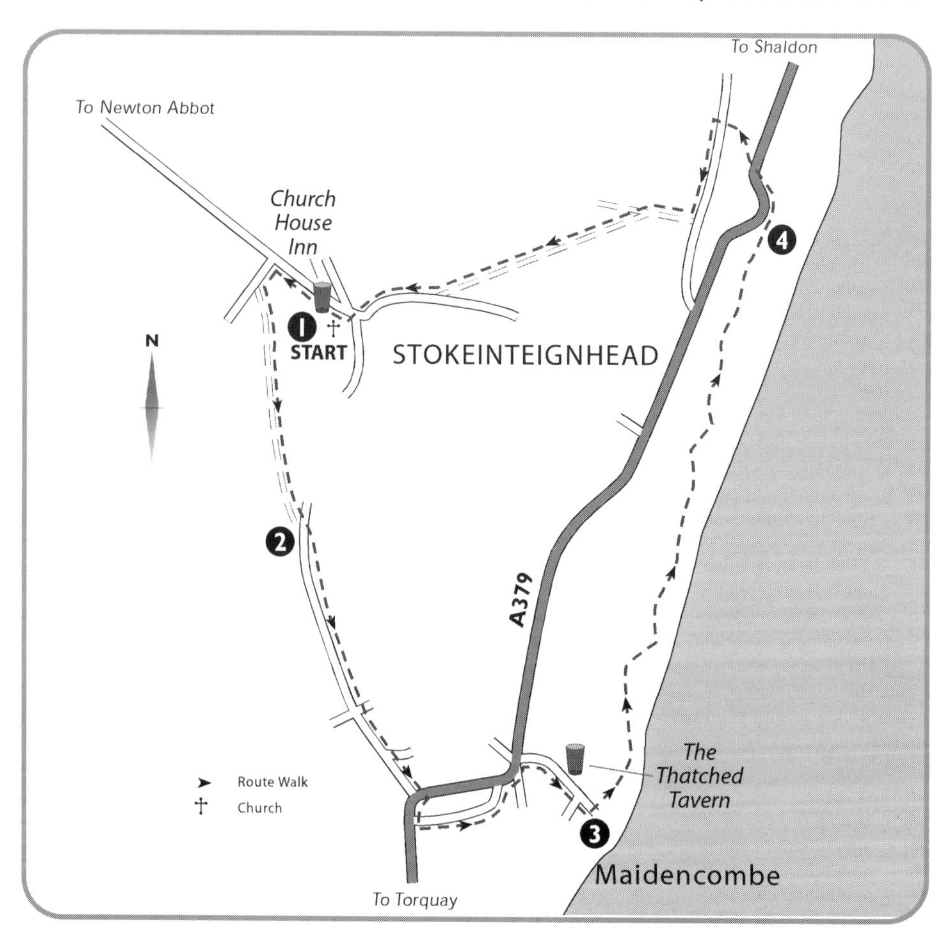

outskirts of Maidencombe and then come out at the main A379. Turn right and after a few yards left down Sladnor Park Road. It swings left and left again and comes out at the A379 again. Turn right and follow the road for 200 yards, until you come to a lane going left to Stokeinteignhead and two lanes on the right in quick succession. Take the second of these and follow it down a steep hill to the lovely little village of Maidencombe. At the junction, go straight on. If you fancy a refreshment stop at this point, the Thatched Tavern is on your left. *(1¼ miles)*

❸ At the bottom is the beach car park; turn left just before you reach it, along a track. Towards the end you will see a Coast Path waymark pointing left; follow the path it indicates to a stile. It passes above some houses and then swings left, right and left again, around a field. It continues to skirt fields on the left, with a hedge and bank separating it from the cliff on the right for about a mile. It dips and climbs to cross the deep valleys along the way. Ignore the path going left to the main road after about ½ mile, and continue along the Coast Path. Soon after you will see Teignmouth along the coast ahead of you.

After a further ½ mile you will see another path on the left; ignore that as well. Shortly after you will cross a stile and, instead of skirting the fields on the left, the path now crosses two fields, continuing to climb and descend. It goes steeply down to a small copse, still hugging the cliff edge. Two more climbs, with a short descent in between, bring you to the A379 again. *(2 miles)*

❹ Turn right and follow the road for 250 yards, initially along a pavement and then along a path separated from the road by a bank. When the path turns right, keep following the road. Take care as there is no pavement or path here. After 100 yards you will see a gap in the bushes on the left, with a public footpath sign; turn off and follow the rather overgrown path to a gate and then to a stile. It goes half left between fences to another stile. The path then goes left to a third stile and a lane; turn left.

As you follow this lane, look to your right for a superb view up the River Teign to Dartmoor. You climb gently and when you reach the brow of the hill you will see a green lane on your right; turn along it. You now have the whole valley in front of you, stretching up to Dartmoor. After 250 yards the green lane forks; go left and as you follow this lane down you will see Stokeinteignhead below. After a little more than ½ mile you emerge onto a lane; bear right and follow it into the village. The Church House Inn is immediately in front of you at the T-junction in the centre of the village. *(1¾ miles)*

Date walk completed:

....

Places of Interest Nearby

Torquay, about 3½ miles away, has a wide variety of tourist attractions. At Shaldon, 2 miles in the other direction, you will find the **Shaldon Wildlife Trust**, a small zoo that specialises in breeding endangered species. Telephone: 01626 872234.

Walk 17 # Lutton

The Mountain Inn

From the pretty villages of Lutton and Cornwood, this lovely ramble takes you via lanes and tracks to the wide open spaces of Dartmoor. The return leg is along attractive forest tracks, with magnificent rhododendrons on either side. The views from the moor are superb, although some effort is needed to enjoy them to the full – but if you would prefer to avoid both the effort and the views, there is a short cut.

The name of the welcoming **Mountain Inn** is a corruption of Lord Mourtain, a 17th-century landowner. It was converted from two cottages, one of which was already a cider and ale house. There are bare stone walls and low beams, a cosy bar with an open fireplace, a small, comfortable lounge with a pedal organ in one corner and a wood-burning stove, and a terrace. The food is all home-cooked, using local produce wherever possible, and ranges from soups and snacks such as brie bites and the celebrated rare roast beef baguettes to chicken and steak dishes.

Telephone: *01752 837247.*

Distance: *5½ miles*

OS Explorer OL28 Dartmoor
GR 596594 (pub), 594596 (parking)

A fairly easy walk for most of its length, but with one long, steady and occasionally rough climb in the middle (which can be avoided if required – see point 3 of the route description)

Starting point: There is limited parking in Lutton, so it is best to use the parking area at the top of Gibb Hill, just beyond the cattle grid. That is where the route starts. The pub car park is very small, so please do not leave your car there while walking.

How to get there: From the north-east, leave the A38 at Lee Mill and follow the signs for Cornwood. Turn left in the centre of the village, following the sign for Lutton. In Lutton, turn right up Mountain Hill, which leads to Old Chapel Road. From the south-west, leave at the Deep Lane junction and follow the signs for Sparkwell and then for Lutton. Turn left up Old Chapel Road. From Old Chapel Road turn north up Gibb Hill and cross the cattle grid at the top to park.

The Walk

❶ Cross the cattle grid below the parking area and follow the lane on the other side down into Lutton. At the junction, where the main lane goes right, bear left down a narrower lane. At the bottom turn left and you will find the Mountain Inn on your left after about 100 yards. Continue left beyond the pub, following the lane down to a road; turn left. After about ½ mile you come to the attractive village of Cornwood. Continue along the road you are on until you reach a crossroads, with the Cornwood Inn on your right. *(1 mile)*

❷ Go straight across (signposted to Torr and Harford). After ¼ mile you will find another lane on your left; turn up it. This is a pretty stretch, fringed with hedgerows and with virtually no traffic. The lane climbs gently, and towards the top goes round to the right and then to the left. You come to a junction, with

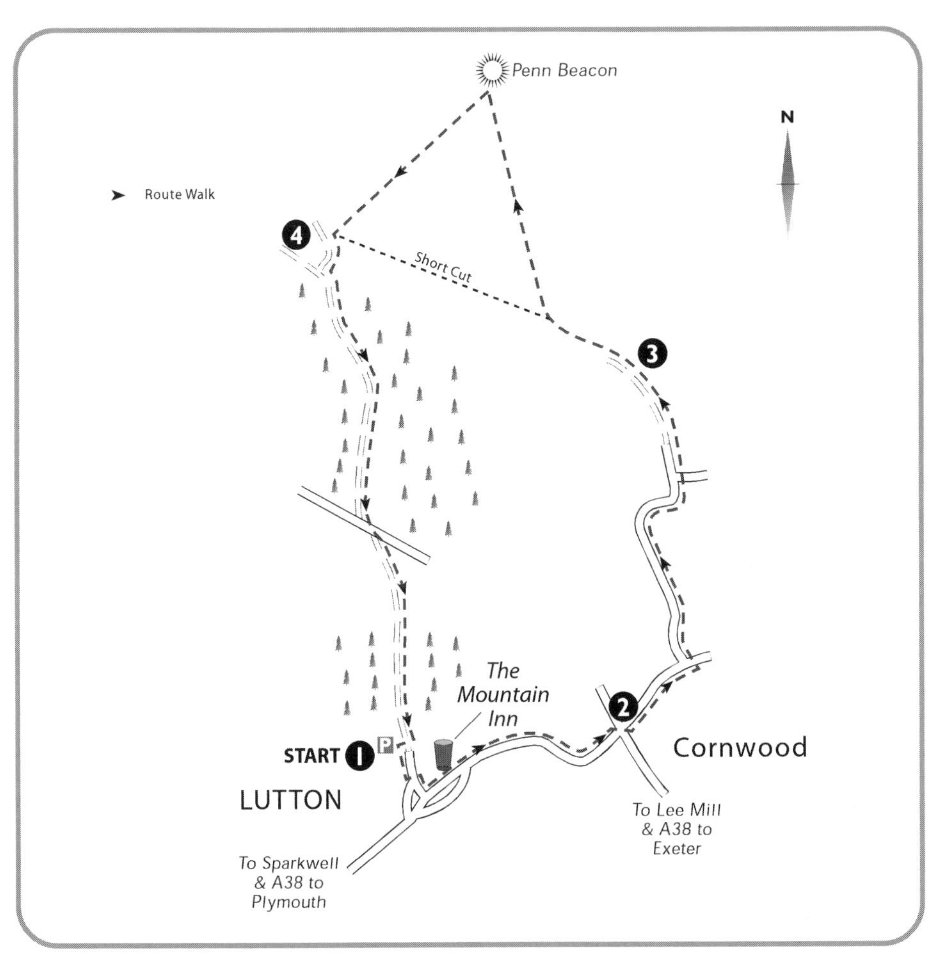

another lane going right; carry straight on. After a while the surfaced lane becomes a track and continues to climb gently. It eventually ends at a gate leading onto the open moor. *(1¼ miles)*

❸ Follow the wall on your left until it bends left. Here you have a choice. The main route takes you up across the moor for a mile to Penn Beacon; if you would prefer to avoid the climb, you can turn left and follow the wall to its end, keeping to the low ground, and rejoin the main route at point 4. However, you will miss the stunning view if you do.

The main route follows the path that goes half left. It will bring you to a broader track; go left along it and follow it as it bends right to cross a leat. It becomes less clear as you follow it up, but it is still discernible. Look back as you go for the start of the views – a lovely panorama across South Devon, with Plymouth to the west. The track eventually peters out, but by the time it does you can see your objective – Penn Beacon on the horizon with a cairn at the top. When you get there, the panorama is stunning – almost through 360 degrees, with just Shell Top to the north obscuring the view in that direction. To the west you can see the moonscape-like excavations of the Lee Moor china clay quarry.

Turn left and head back down the hill. There is no path, but the going is easy and if you aim to the left of the grassed spoil tip below you will be walking in the right direction. Halfway down you pass a large cairn and at the bottom you meet a wall. Turn right along it and follow it to its end, crossing a wall via a ladder stile towards the end. *(1½ miles)*

A drove road near Cornwood

❹ At the end, you clamber over some rocks and go down to a track. Turn left and follow the track round to the right, with a china clay quarry on your right. At the junction go left and follow the track round to the right. It enters a conifer plantation, with rhododendrons alongside. You emerge via a cattle grid onto a road; turn left and after a short distance right along another track, marked with a public bridleway sign. This takes you across a stretch of heathland and into another conifer plantation. It emerges again alongside a house, with the parking area beyond. *(1¾ miles)*

Date walk completed:

....

Places of Interest Nearby

About a mile down the road, near Sparkwell, is the **Dartmoor Wildlife Park**. Telephone: 01752 837209. Ten miles away is **Plymouth**, with its historic **Barbican** area and a variety of attractions, including the **National Marine Aquarium** and the **Dome**, which has displays of the city's history.

The Churston Court Inn

Despite its proximity to busy Torquay and Paignton, this is a delightfully peaceful walk. It is also very varied, taking in a stretch of the Torbay coast, rolling countryside and the majestic River Dart. Some of the views, up and down the river and across the bay, are quite outstanding. And halfway round, there is the opportunity, with a short detour, to visit the National Trust's Greenway, a beautiful garden that time seems to have passed by, on the banks of the Dart.

Distance: *5½ miles*

OS Explorer OL20 South Devon
GR 904563

A moderate walk along mainly flat terrain, but with one or two hills

Starting point: The Churston Court Inn. You can leave your car in the inn car park with permission; otherwise park in the road approaching the village from the main road. Alternatively, park in the Broadsands pay and display car park and start the walk at point 2.

How to get there: Turn north off the A3022 between Paignton and Brixham at Churston Ferrers, following the signs for Churston Village. When the road bends sharp right, turn left, following the sign for the Churston Court Inn, which you will find alongside the church.

The lovely old **Churston Court Inn**, a favourite haunt of Agatha Christie, was originally a Saxon manor house, and still has features from that era, including two large halls (now the bar and restaurant), the original windows and tapestries on the walls. There are also several small, secluded rooms behind the two main ones, and two beer gardens outside. The inn, which once served as a monastery, is said to be haunted by the ghost of a monk. Open all day, it offers a wide range of fare, from bar snacks to main meals, including fish (naturally) and vegetarian dishes, with a mouthwatering specials board.

Telephone: *01803 842186.*

The Walk

❶ Turn left and follow the lane round the church. At the junction go straight on (signposted to Links Close). At the end turn right and immediately left, down a path signposted to the beach. Cross a golf course and follow the path through some trees; at the junction go straight on and you will come to a kissing-gate. Go through and turn right. At a T-junction turn right and when the path forks bear left. Go through a kissing-gate onto a large grassed area. Go through another kissing-gate at the end and you will find Broadsands beach ahead of you. Turn left to the car park. *(1 mile)*

❷ On the other side of the car park turn right into a road and follow it as it winds up and passes under a viaduct. Just beyond it swings right. As it does so, about 50 yards from the viaduct, turn left off the road, following the public footpath sign. After a few yards the path twists to the right and comes out at a road; turn right and almost immediately left, following the waymark. After 50 yards or so you come to a main road; cross over and go half left across the

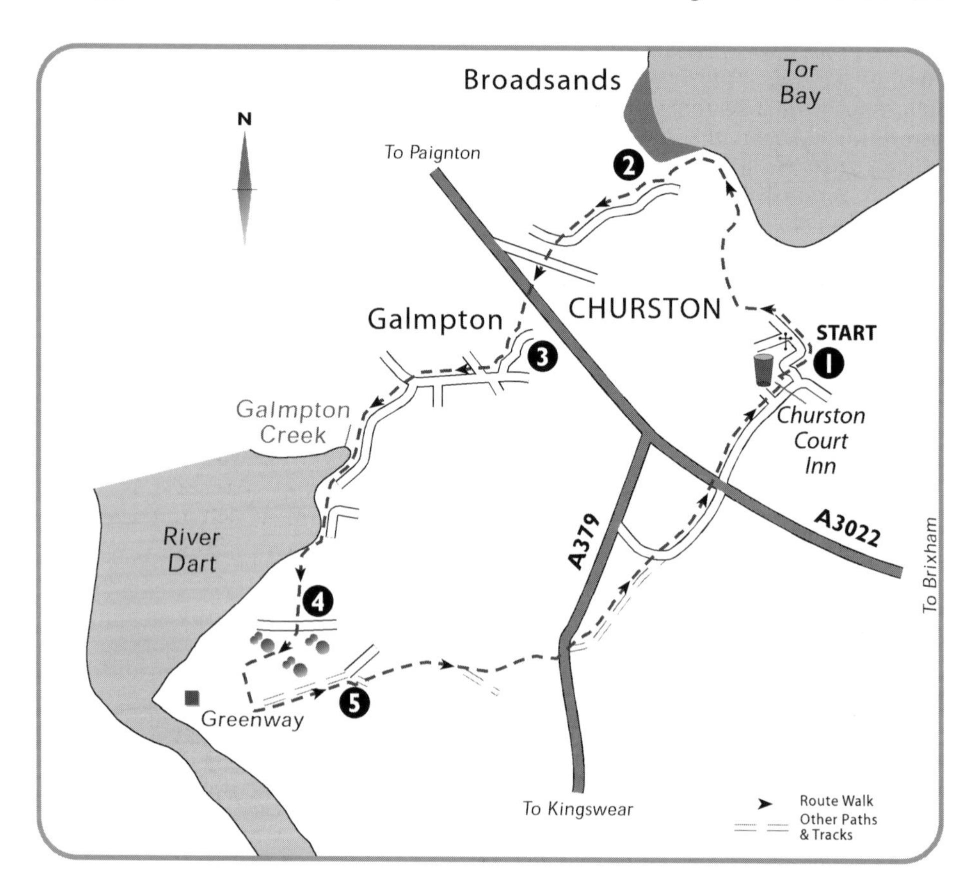

grassy stretch on the other side to reach a lane. Follow that down into the village of Galmpton. At the T-junction, turn right into Stoke Gabriel Road. *(3/4 mile)*

3 Follow this road out of Galmpton, and on the outskirts turn left down Kiln Road. You pass an old limekiln and then some industrial units. Go straight on, following the waymark for the Torbay and Dart Link. When you come to the entrance to Cliff Cottage, bear left along a path, again following the Torbay and Dart Link waymark.

The path joins another lane; go straight on downhill. Just before you reach a house turn right off the lane and continue along the river shoreline, following the public footpath sign. Just before you reach another limekiln cross a stile on your left and bear right across a field. About halfway up cross another stile in the fence on the right. Follow the fence on the other side to a stone stile leading into a farmyard. Cross the farmyard to a drive; turn right and immediately left to cross another stone stile. Keep to the left of the next field to yet another stone stile. *(1 mile)*

4 Cross the lane beyond to a kissing-gate into a wood (signposted to Greenway and the ferry). At the path junction go straight on, climbing up through the wood. At the top, go round to the right to join a track at a sharp bend; take the left-hand route, still climbing. Leave the wood via a gate and keep to the left of the field beyond, through another gate and down a short track. Go through a gateway and turn left (signposted to Maypool and Kingswear). Alternatively, you can turn half right to visit the gardens at Greenway.

Go through two gates in quick succession and turn left after the second (signposted to Maypool and Kingswear again). Go along the top of a field to a gate, and follow the track on the other side, passing some houses and a hotel. (3/4 mile)

5 Just beyond the hotel turn right onto a track, signposted to Kingswear. Just beyond Greenway Barton turn left and cross a stile. Follow the track on the other side to a field; keep to the left-hand side. At the end of the field, cross a stile and follow a path. When the path joins a track go straight on, and after a few yards cross a stile on your left. Turn half right down the field beyond and round a dip at the bottom. Follow the path across the field to a stile; cross the next field to another stile and onto a busy road.

Turn left and almost immediately right down a green lane that eventually emerges onto a lane. Carry straight on to another main road; cross it to another road, leading through Churston Ferrers. You go under a railway line, and about 150 yards further on the road bends right; as it does so, go left to return to the Churston Court Inn. *(2 miles)*

Date walk completed:

....

Places of Interest Nearby

In Paignton (2½ miles), is the **Quay West water park**, with flumes, slides and other delights. Telephone: 01803 555550. **Churston Station** (3/4 mile) is one of the stops on the **Paignton and Dartmoor Steam Railway**. Telephone: 01803 555872

Walk 19 Wembury

The Odd Wheel

From rolling farmland to spectacular coastal views, from the lovely Yealm estuary to lanes that are flower-fringed for much of the year, this beautiful route is full of variety and interest. Pretty farm paths take you to a river valley, which you follow down to the coast. There you join the South West Coast Path, where you can enjoy a superb panorama, particularly to the west. You follow it to the River Yealm, then turn inland and return to Wembury via a track and farm path.

Distance: *4 miles*

OS Explorer OL20 South Devon
GR 527496

An easy and generally level walk along clear paths; the only climbs are so gentle that one hardly notices them

Starting point: The Odd Wheel. Please ask before leaving your car in the pub car park while walking. There is also plenty of space in Wembury's side roads.

How to get there: Turn south-west off the A379 Plymouth to Kingsbridge road at Elburton, just outside Plymouth, and follow the signs to Wembury. The pub is on the way into the village.

Once a cider house, the **Odd Wheel** derives its name from the wheel set into the outside wall, which has strangely shaped spokes. The pub's main entrance leads into a plain bar with a tiled floor, pool table and darts board. Beyond it is a very comfortable, carpeted lounge, with a view out over the surrounding fields. There is also a small garden with an animal and bird enclosure. 'Real ale and real food' are offered – the latter ranging from sandwiches, snacks and salads to steaks and vegetarian options, as well as daily specials, which might include fare as varied as moussaka and sea bass.

Telephone: *01752 862287.*

The Walk

❶ Turn left and follow Traine Road down into a dip and up the other side. After 150 yards you will pass a gate on your left with a stile just beyond it. Cross the stile, following the footpath sign for Ford and Langdon. Go diagonally right across the field beyond. In the far corner of the field, go through a gap in the hedge to join a track; bear left to follow it.

At the end of the next field go through another gap and turn immediately right to cross a stile. Go diagonally left across the next field; when you get to the far corner, ignore the gate on the left and go through the gap in the hedge on the right. Turn left to skirt the edge of the field. Go through a gap at the end and keep to the left again. Cross a stile at the end and follow the wall on your left down a small hill. *(3/4 mile)*

❷ Turn left along the grassy track at the bottom, through a gap and along the bottom of the next field, with a belt of trees and a stream on your right. Cross a stile at the end and continue along the bottom of the next field to another stile by some houses. At the path junction go right and follow a track between the

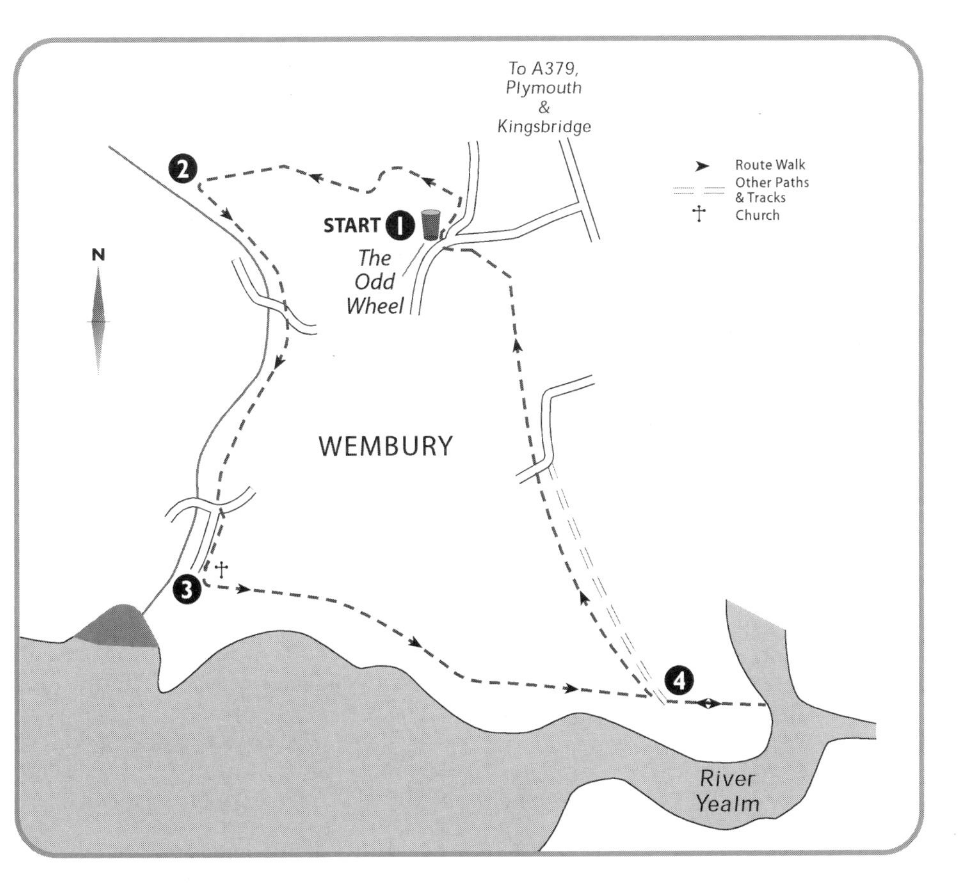

The coast at Wembury

houses to join a lane. Turn left and, after a few yards, right (signposted to Church Road). The sign points through a gate, but it is better to cross the stile to the left of it. This leads to a permissive path that runs parallel to the main bridleway. The latter is often very muddy and churned up by horses, whereas the permissive path avoids these problems.

After 600 yards or so, the two paths converge by a gate and stile. Cross the stile and follow the track on the other side to a drive; bear right. Cross the lane at the end, following the sign for the Erme Plym Trail. Where the lane forks go left to reach the attractive church. Go into the churchyard and round to the right of the church, where you get a lovely view across Wembury Bay to your right and out to the Great Mew Stone. Go through a gate on the other side to reach the Coast Path. *(1 mile)*

❸ Turn left and follow the path as it climbs gently for a while and then levels off. Ignore a footpath going left and continue along the Coast Path. There is another gentle climb, with a seat at the top from which you can admire the views along the coast.

The path now descends to a kissing-gate. Continue along the path on the other side. Soon you will find a farm on your left and the path runs inland for a short distance to cross a small rivulet. Go through another kissing-gate and then a third. Just beyond is a junction. If you continue straight on for about 300 yards or so, you will come to a lovely viewpoint. *(1 mile)*

❹ Turn left at the junction, go through two gates in quick succession and follow the track on the other side. After a little over ½ mile you come to a surfaced lane; go straight on. After another 200 yards the lane swings sharply to the right. Go straight on through a gate (signposted to Knighton) and keep to the right of the field beyond, alongside the high boundary wall of Wembury House. At the end of the field you go through two more kissing-gates. Follow the clear path straight across the next field. At the end go down some steps and turn left alongside some houses. After a few yards turn right. The path emerges at the road into Wembury; turn left and you will see the Odd Wheel 100 yards down the road on your right. *(1¼ miles)*

Date walk completed:

....

Places of Interest Nearby

Plymouth is just 6 miles away, with a wide variety of attractions, including the historic **Barbican** area, the **Mayflower Steps**, from which the Pilgrim Fathers set sail for America, the **Plymouth Dome** (telephone: 01752 603300) which has displays and features on Plymouth's history, and the **National Marine Aquarium** (telephone: 01752 600301).

Thurlestone

The Village Inn

Outstanding views, both across the rich South Hams countryside and along the coast, are the main feature of this walk, but there are other pleasures to enjoy as well. Tracks and farm paths that are often flower-filled take you out to the hamlet of South Huish. From there you head along green lanes, lanes and tracks down to the South West Coast Path, which guides you back to Thurlestone.

***Distance:** 5 3/4 miles*

OS Explorer OL20 South Devon
GR 675429

A moderate walk with some fairly stiff climbing in parts and one rather rough stretch, but if you are suitably clothed and shod, you should not find the going too difficult

Starting point: The Village Inn. Please ask before leaving your car in the pub car park while walking. Some parking is possible in the road through the village, but only between October and March. Alternatively, the golf club, on the southern edge of the village, offers public parking (pay at the golf club; you would then start the walk at point 5).

How to get there: Turn south off the A379 Plymouth to Kingsbridge road at the big roundabout just west of Churchstow, and follow the signs to Thurlestone.

The 16th-century stone-built **Village Inn** started out as a farmhouse, and was converted into a hotel at the end of the 19th century. The hotel accommodation was eventually transferred to what became the four-star Thurlestone Hotel, leaving the original building as an attractive hostelry in its own right. It has one long, pleasantly decorated bar, with a large fireplace. The walls are panelled, and wooden half-partitions provide snug little alcoves. The mouthwatering fare ranges from interesting soups (carrot and cumin was on the menu when I last visited), jacket potatoes and filled baguettes to a variety of main courses, including several seafood specialities.

Telephone: 01548 560382.

The Walk

❶ Turn right and follow the lane through the village. You will pass a lane going left, and about 100 yards further on you will see another going right, marked with a public footpath sign pointing to Whitlocksworthy. Turn off here and follow the lane to a T-junction; turn left, and when the road bends to the left turn right across a stile, following the footpath sign. Go straight across the field beyond.

Cross another stile at the end of the field and go left and then right to skirt the next field. At the end of this field cross a stone footbridge and go through a kissing-gate. Keep to the right of the next field to another stile, and go right and then left to skirt the field on the other side. Halfway up go right, following the waymark, to join a track. At the junction go left and you will emerge at the junction of two lanes. *(1 mile)*

❷ Cross the first lane and turn left at the second. After 50 yards turn right down a surfaced track, following the footpath sign. At the gates at the end go left across a stile onto a narrow footpath. You cross

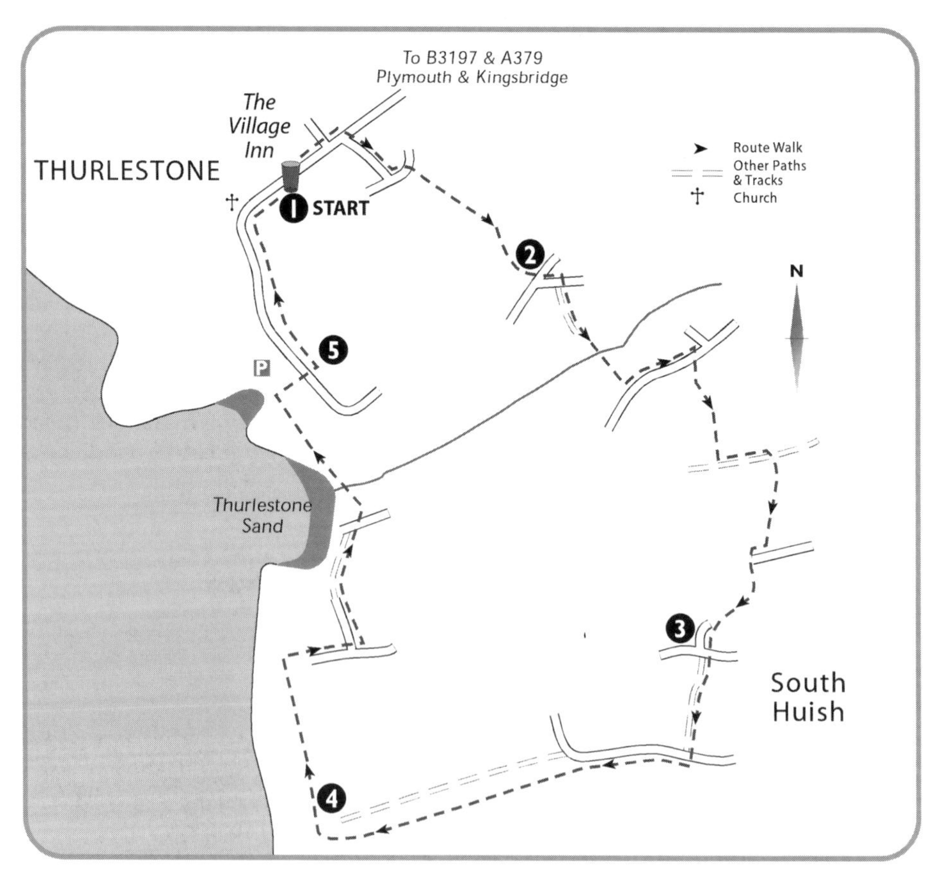

a footbridge and the path crosses the marshes of South Milton Ley. On the other side you cross another footbridge and then another stile. Keep to the left of a field to yet another stile, which leads into a wood. You emerge onto a lane; turn left.

After 300 yards, as the lane swings left, turn right through a gate (signposted to South Huish). Follow the grassy track on the other side as it skirts round to the right of a field. There follows a fairly stiff climb. You go through a gap in the hedge and continue climbing along the right-hand edge of the next field. Go through a gap at the end and bear left, keeping the next hedge on your right. At the end, a stile takes you onto a green lane; turn left.

After 200 yards turn right across another stile, following the footpath sign, and keep to the left of the next field. At the end of the field, cross a stile and continue to keep to the left. Turn left at the bottom and cross a stile. Keep to the left on the other side and go through a gate onto a lane; turn right. You pass some houses, and on the other side you will find a stile on your left; cross it and keep to the left of a field. At the end cross a footbridge and a stile and go diagonally right across the next field to another stile. Turn left on the other side and pass a house to reach a lane; follow that to a T-junction. *(1½ miles)*

❸ Cross over to a green lane. This can be a bit overgrown, but it is quite passable and becomes better further along. It is, however, somewhat rough underfoot, so take care. You come out onto a lane; turn right. After ¼ mile the lane turns sharp right; go straight on down a track. After a little over ¼ mile the track becomes a path, which goes down to meet the South West Coast Path. *(1¼ miles)*

❹ Turn right and go through a kissing-gate. Go through another kissing-gate and join a lane. At the junction turn left (signposted as the Coast Path to Thurlestone). The lane becomes a track and passes a car park. On the other side it joins another lane; as it does so, turn left, again following the Coast Path sign for Thurlestone. The path goes right and then left to cross a stream and some reed beds. It then joins another lane. Where that goes right, go straight on along a path, following the Coast Path acorn sign. You join another lane and soon the Thurlestone Golf Club comes into view. When it does, look out for a post with a waymark pointing right. Turn off the Coast Path here and follow the path to the car park. *(1¼ miles)*

❺ Turn left through the car park and out onto the lane beyond. Turn left and follow the lane into Thurlestone. Soon after it swings right you will find the pub on your right. *(¾ mile)*

Date walk completed:

....

Place of Interest Nearby

Five miles away, just outside Kingsbridge, is **Sorley Tunnel Adventure Farm**, which includes a children's play area as well as a range of farm animals. Telephone: 01548 854078.

Walk 21 Bude

The Falcon Inn

The north Cornish coast, with its rugged headlands, quiet coves and long, sandy beaches, offers some truly spectacular views, and this walk enables you to enjoy them without too much effort. After exploring Bude's canal basin, the route joins the South West Coast Path. A long stretch along the cliffs follows, with panoramas around Bude Bay and along the coast beyond. Farm paths then take you inland to the canal, where you join the pretty towpath for the return to Bude.

***Distance:** 5½ miles*

OS Explorer 111 Bude, Boscastle and Tintagel
GR 206061

A fairly easy walk over good terrain, with no steep climbs

Starting point: The Falcon Inn. The car park is alongside the Bude Canal and there is no objection to customers leaving their cars there while they walk (but please ask first). There is also a public pay and display car park on the other side of the canal.

How to get there: Turn west off the main A39 and head for the town centre. Follow the signs to the canal and cross it. The Falcon Inn is on the right and the car park on the left.

The **Falcon Inn** is part of the impressive Falcon Hotel, a 19th century coaching house which sits alongside the Bude Canal in a particularly attractive part of town. It comprises two interconnected lounges. Both are decorated with old photographs and are comfortable, light and airy. There is a beer terrace in the front, overlooking the canal and the inner harbour. The bar food is wide ranging and delicious. The fish is particularly good, but salads, steaks and bar snacks are also available, as well as more exotic offerings such as Cajun chicken. Local real ales are featured.

***Telephone:** 01288 352005.*

The Walk

❶ Turn left as you leave the Falcon and follow the small road that runs alongside the canal, which is signposted to the breakwater. Follow it round to the left at the end of the canal, and when it ends, climb some steps to a kissing-gate. Turn right on the other side (signposted as the Coast Path to Widemouth Bay). As you go, you can look down to your right over Summerleaze Beach across the River Neet. When you get close to the cliff edge, bear left, following the Coast Path waymark. You soon come to Compass Point, with its octagonal tower showing the directions of the different points of the compass. *(½ mile)*

❷ Carry on past it and you immediately get a magnificent view around Bude Bay and down the coast. You will come to a kissing-gate on the left; go through it and turn right to follow the edge of the cliff. As you go the view up ahead becomes even better, and you can see all the way

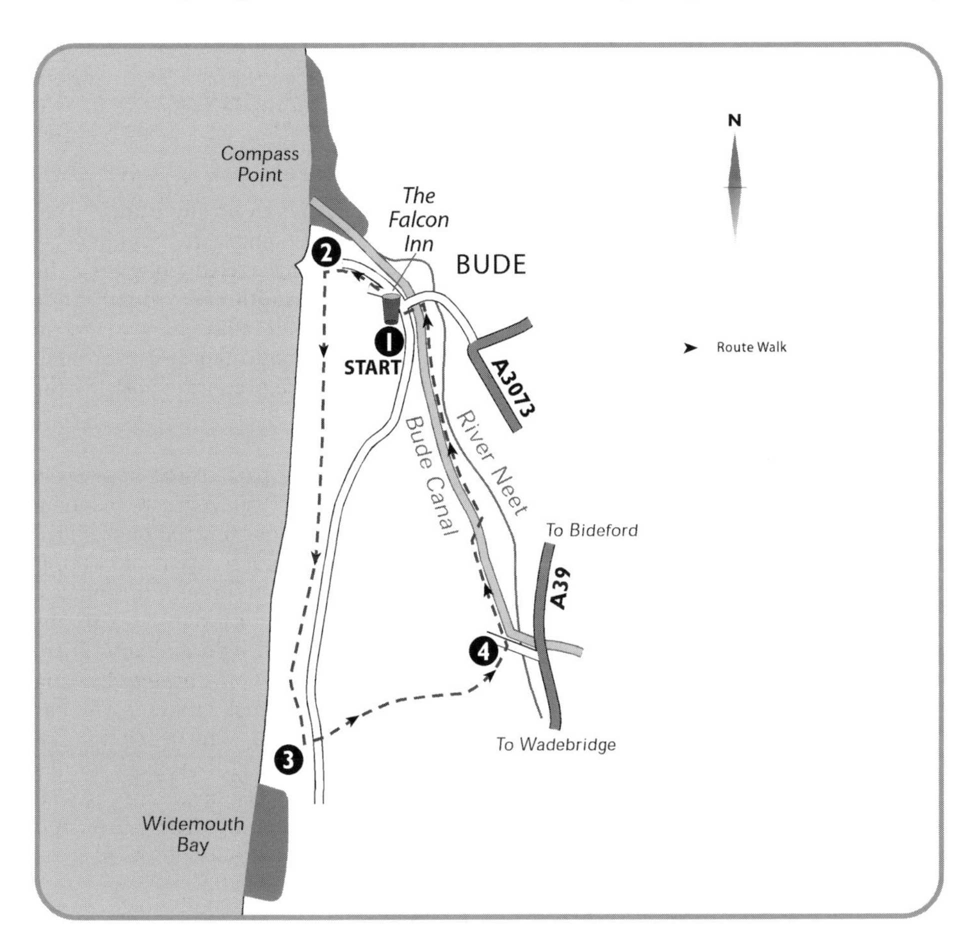

along to Trevose Head – a vista that will stay with you for almost 2 miles. Looking back you get an almost equally good view the other way, with Lundy in the distance. You come to a gateway followed by a gentle hill. Go through a kissing-gate at the top and carry on along the cliff. The area to the right is a pink mass of thrift in summer.

At the end of this field you go through another kissing-gate and follow a path alongside some houses. You come out at a road; the path runs alongside it for a while and then veers away from it. As it does so, the wide expanse of Widemouth Sand comes into view. Shortly afterwards you will see a car park ahead of you; the Coast Path runs round the headland on the right, but if you prefer you can simply cut across past the car park. A little way beyond the car park you will come to a house; turn left up its drive. *(2 miles)*

❸ Follow the drive to the road and cross over to a stile. Bear left in the field beyond. When you reach the hedge at the edge of the field, follow it to the right. At the end go through a gate and bear left on the other side. At the end of that field, cross a stile and keep to the right of the next field. Cross another stile and bear left. There is yet another stile at the end of this field; follow the track on the other side as it curves round to the left. Another stile takes you into a lane; turn right. (If you fancy some refreshment at this point in the walk, the Woodland Tea Garden on the left has a varied menu.) Just before the lane crosses the canal, cross a stile on the left. *(1¼ miles)*

The Bude canal

❹ Keep to the left of a field to another stile, on the other side of which is a surfaced path alongside the Bude Canal. This canal was built in the 1820s to transport the chemical-rich Bude sand inland to fertilise the rather poor agricultural soil of the hinterland. It is very pretty along here, with a small wood on the left and the canal on the right. Soon the wood gives way to fields, which are covered in buttercups and yellow iris in summer. You come to a lane that crosses the canal; cross with it and turn left on the other side to follow the opposite bank. You now have the River Neet on your right, and just before you reach Bude you will find a hide from which you can watch the birds on the river. Once in the town you pass the public car park on your right and come to a road. Turn left to cross the canal and return to the Falcon. *(1¾ miles)*

Date walk completed:

....

Place of Interest Nearby

At Kilkhampton, about 4 miles north of Bude, there is **Brocklands Adventure Park**, with rides, an assault course, a soft play area and other children's attractions. Telephone: 01288 321920.

Boscastle 22 Walk

The Napoleon Inn

Distance: 6¾ miles

OS Explorer 111 Bude, Boscastle and Tintagel
GR 099906

A challenging walk with several steep hills, especially along the Coast Path, and many of the farm paths can be muddy

Starting point: The Napoleon Inn. The pub car park is very small, so please do not leave your car there while walking. It should be possible to find parking in the road, or use the free public car park at the bottom of the village and start the walk there.

How to get there: Boscastle is on the coast, west of the A39 Bude to Wadebridge road. From the south, take the B3266 and you will see the pub in High Street on the left just after you enter the village. From the north, take the B3263, go through the village and turn left at the top of the hill (signposted to Camelford). High Street is on the right after 150 yards.

This is a superb and varied walk. It includes agricultural uplands with panoramic views out to sea, the delightful, wooded St Nectan's Glen, a stretch of the South West Coast Path along rugged cliff tops and the pretty village of Boscastle itself, with its harbour and old slate houses.

The **Napoleon** is a gem of a pub, decorated throughout with pictures of the Napoleonic wars. It is a 15th-century stone building with several rooms on different levels, all with slate floors and oak beams, and most with fireplaces. The main bar has settles and tables, and there is also a snug and what is called the fun bar, which has games. A large garden is outside, also a covered terrace. The bar menu ranges from pasties, soup and baguettes to a range of fish, chicken, steak and vegetarian specials. Local produce is used wherever possible. The restaurant, Boney's Bistro, has its own menu.

Telephone: 01840 250204.

The Walk

❶ Turn right as you leave the pub and follow High Street up the hill. At the crossroads 100 yards up the street turn right along Paradise Road. It swings to the right after 150 yards; follow it round. Then, after another 250 yards, it swings right again; this time turn left up a surfaced drive for Trerosewill Farmhouse. Pass the farmhouse and follow the track to the right and then after a few yards to the left. Just after the left turn go right across a stone stile. Bear left to follow the right-hand fence across a field to another stone stile. Bear left across the next field. Cross a third stone stile and keep to the left of the next field, following the curve of the hedge. Where the hedge goes sharply left, go straight across to a gap in the bank ahead. Turn left immediately beyond it and cross a footbridge and a stile. Bear right on the other side to climb up the field to a gate. Beyond it take the grassy track, to the left of a field, to a lane. *(1 mile)*

❷ Turn right and then after 50 yards left down another grassy track and immediately right across a stone stile, following the public footpath sign. Go diagonally across a field to a lane. Do not cross the stile into the lane, however, but take the one on the left into another field. Cut straight across that field to a stone stile into the lane at a bend; bear left and follow the lane down a hill. After 200 yards look out for some steps and a stile on the right; the public footpath sign is not visible from the lane. Cross a small

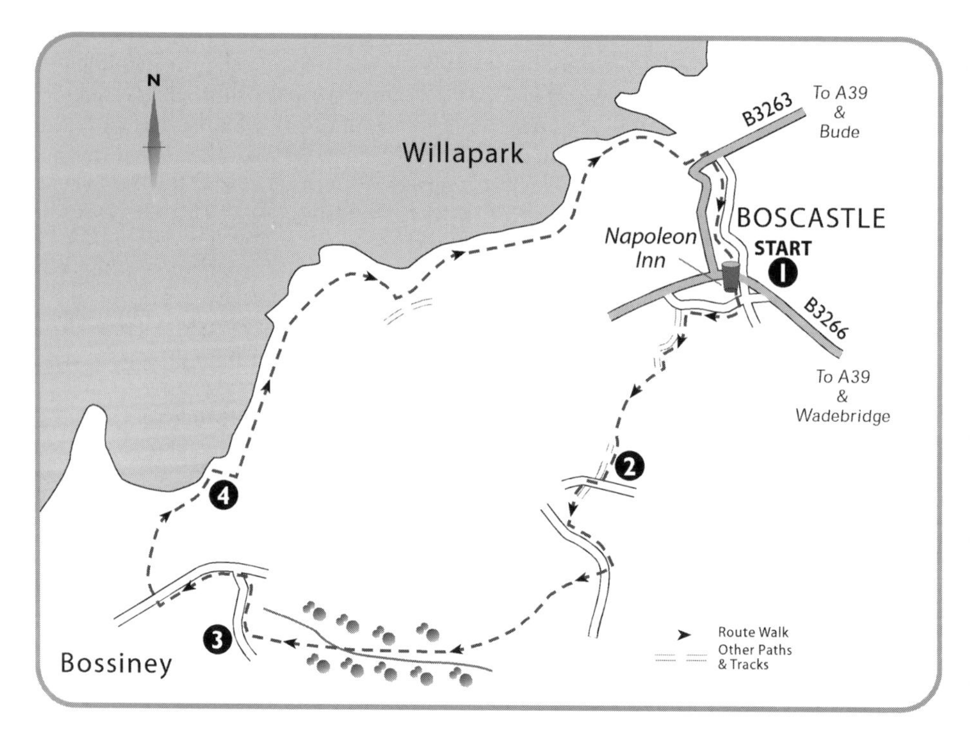

The view from Firebeacon Hill

field to two stiles separated by a bank and bear right across another small field to two more stiles separated by a footbridge. Keep to the left of the next field and after a few yards you will see another footbridge and stiles on the left. Cross and turn right alongside the river you have just crossed. Go over another stile into a belt of trees before crossing the river again.

Turn left to follow the stream and cross yet another stile. At the end of the next field is a gate; go round a ruined farm building and cross another field to another two stiles. Cross three more fields, passing through gaps in the banks that separate them, and cross a stile at the end of the third. The path now goes to the right around the Waterfall Tea Garden and immediately beyond the tea garden gate it goes left to take you through a pretty wood above the river and then down some steps to meet it. You are now in St Nectan's Glen, a delightful wooded valley. Follow the path through the trees alongside the river to a footbridge on the left. Cross it and then, after 50 yards, cross back to the other side of the river via a smaller footbridge. After 150 yards you should come to a third bridge, with a fork in the path. Cross back to the left-hand bank, following the sign for Halgabron. (Note: This bridge was washed away in the floods of 2004. If it has still not been replaced when you walk this route, retrace your steps to the previous bridge and make your way downstream on the left bank to join the path.) Climb through the wood, away from the river, and leave it via a kissing-gate. Bear left across a field to a wooden stile followed by a stone stile into a lane; turn right. *(1¾ miles)*

❸ Follow the lane down for about 500 yards to a T-junction; turn left. Follow this road for another 500 yards, and as you reach the outskirts of Bossiney you will see a sign on the right, pointing to the Coast Path. Turn off here and go through a gate into a field. Bear right over the brow of a hill and follow the Coast Path running along the edge of the cliff below you. Bear right. *(1 mile)*

❹ Follow the path along the cliff top. After 500 yards or so it swings inland and goes down steep steps to meet Rocky Valley. Cross a footbridge over the river at the bottom and climb more steep steps on the other side. The path goes over a headland and runs along the cliff, crossing the odd wall on the way. About ¾ mile beyond Rocky Valley the path rounds Firebeacon Hill and meets a track. Turn left and then as the track bends right into a field, turn off left, following the Coast Path acorn waymark. After another 250 yards you cross a stone stile into a field; keep to the left and then follow the fence round to the right. Cross a boardwalk and follow the path down steeply to the left.

Cross a stream and climb some more steep steps on the other side. Go through a gate at the top and then a stile. More steps take you to Forrabury Common. You pass Willapark, with its white watchtower, on your left and then, as you round a headland, Boscastle harbour comes into view. Follow the path along the top of the valley to a road and turn left. The road takes you down the hill into the village; at the bottom turn right up Old Road. Pass the Wellington Hotel and climb a long, straight hill. After 500 yards the road swings left and becomes Dunn Street as it passes the post office. It then swings right and comes out at a crossroads; go straight across for High Street and the pub. *(3 miles)*

Date walk completed:

....

Places of Interest Nearby

At the bottom of Boscastle there is the **Museum of Witchcraft**, which has exhibits of witchcraft-related artefacts and regalia (telephone 01749 674712). Three miles down the coast is the village of Tintagel, the legendary birthplace of King Arthur. There you can visit the ruins of **Tintagel Castle**, an English Heritage property (telephone 01840 770328) and the National Trust's **Old Post Office**, a medieval manor house (telephone 01840 770024).

Camelford 23 Walk

The Masons' Arms

The outward leg of this walk skirts the edge of Bodmin Moor, and there are several opportunities to enjoy its grandeur. There are also extensive views to the sea in the other direction and across the patchwork of farmland to the south. Most of the route follows farm paths, but there are also a few pretty lanes and two delightful riverside stretches.

Distance: *7 miles*

OS Explorer 109 Bodmin Moor
GR 106838 (pub) 107838 (car park)

A moderate to easy walk, with just a few climbs and little rough ground

Starting point: The public pay and display car park at the northern end of the town. The pub has no car park.

How to get there: Camelford is on the A39 Bude to Wadebridge road and the starting point is the first car park on the right-hand side as you approach from Bude, the second on the left if you are coming from Wadebridge. The Masons' Arms is about 50 yards down the road.

The 18th-century **Masons' Arms** oozes character. There are two rooms: an attractive, carpeted lounge and a public bar with games. The former has exposed stone walls and low beams displaying a variety of beer mugs, old bottles and teacups. There are also display cases on the walls with a fascinating collection of old objects ranging from Alka Seltzer boxes and Andrews' Liver Salt tins to toys. At the back is a very pretty beer garden. The pub serves a wide variety of dishes, from sandwiches and ploughman's lunches to steaks and fish dishes.

Telephone: 01840 213309.

The Walk

❶ Turn right from the car park and then immediately left along College Road. After about 500 yards, where the lane forks, go straight on across a stone stile. Cross the field beyond to another stone stile, followed by a footbridge. Cross a small field to a stile and a gate and walk up the next field and to the right of the wall at the top. Go through a gate onto a track. The track emerges onto a lane; turn left. After about 700 yards it ends. *(1 mile)*

❷ Turn right through a white gate onto a track. Go past a farm to another gate into a field; keep to the right. At the end there are three gates; go through the left-hand one and follow a track. Go through another gate and keep to the right again. At the end of the field cross three stiles and go straight across the next field, at the end of which there are two stiles. Cross another field and then a farmyard to a gate into lane.

Cross the lane to another gate. Go across the next field, keeping to the right of the cairns. Cross a stile and go over the field beyond. In the far left-hand corner you will find another stile; cross that and two more in quick succession. Keep to the left of the next field, alongside a stream, going across the ends of two walls. Cross a stile into a lane and turn left. At the T-junction turn right. *(1½ miles)*

❸ After about ¾ mile look out for two public footpath signs, one pointing left and one right. Go left, crossing a stile and bearing left alongside a bank. When the bank swings left, cross to a post with a yellow waymark and then follow an overgrown ruined wall down a hill to some trees. Go down some steps and cross some stepping stones. Turn right on the other side and follow the path to a footbridge. Climb up the field on the other side to a stile. Cut across the next field to a gap in the wall and bear left to follow a track through another field. Go over two stiles and emerge at the junction of two lanes.

Cross both lanes and bear right after the second to a stile. Bear left on the other side and cross four fields, keeping left all the time. After the fourth, follow the path through some trees, at the end of

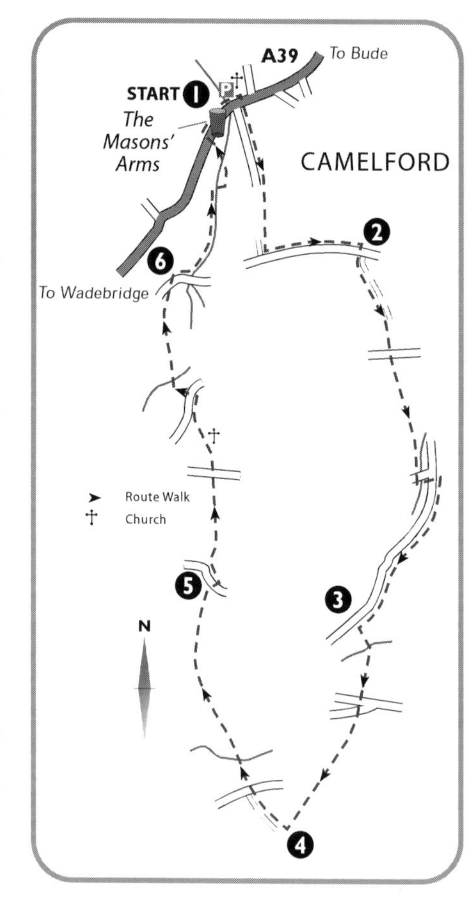

which one more stile and some steps will take you down to a track. *(1 mile)*

❹ Turn right and follow the track through a gate and between farm buildings. The track emerges onto a lane; cross over and climb some stone steps on the other side. A stile takes you into a field; go straight down to a footbridge. Bear left on the other side and climb a hill; do not take the path that goes sharp left to follow the stream. You join a rough track; bear left. Towards the top the track becomes two paths; take the left-hand one and go through a gap in a wall. Keep to the right across two fields and go through a gate on the right at the end of the second. Turn left to another gate. Keep to the right of the next field and go through a gate onto a track.

Bear left and cross a yard between houses to a gate; go through and pass some more buildings to reach a stile. Follow the path round to a stone stile on the right. Cross the field on the other side to a wall and follow it to a gap. Keep to the left of the next field and you will find yourself between two banks. Go through a gate and continue to a track. Follow that through another gate to a lane. *(1¼ miles)*

❺ Turn left and after 100 yards, as the lane swings left, turn sharp right through a gate following the public footpath sign. Turn left on the other side and follow the field boundary to another gate. Follow a track for a short distance and then go right up some steps to a gate. Halfway along the next field you will see a break in the fence on the left with a stile and a yellow waymark. Cross the stile and bear right. Go through a gate in the far corner and then turn right to cross a stile. Turn left on the other side and at the end cross a stone stile. Follow the left-hand boundary of the next field round to the right. After about 50 yards, cross a stile on the left and two more.

Go straight across the field to another stile leading into a lane. Cross to some steps and then a stile. Go straight across the field on the other side to another stile on the left. Cross it and follow the path around Advent church. Leave the churchyard via a gate and cross a stile. Keep to the right on the other side to reach a stile on your right. Cross it and bear left. Pass a pool and cross another stile into a lane; bear right.

After about 200 yards you will see a footpath sign on the left; cross a stile and go down the left-hand side of a field. At the end follow the path to the right and cross a footbridge. Bear right, following the green waymark. At the top climb some steps to a stile. Follow the path on the other side. Cross another stone stile and finally a gate takes you onto a lane. *(1¼ miles)*

❻ Turn right down the hill. Just before you get to the river turn left, and go down some steps. Keep to the right of a meadow. Go through three kissing-gates and you come to a footbridge on the right. Cross it and turn left on the other side. After a short distance cross the river again. The path swings away between houses and through an arch into Camelford's main street. Turn right and you will find the Masons' Arms about 250 yards along. The car park is about 50 yards beyond it. *(1 mile)*

Date walk completed:

....

Walk **24** *Fivelanes*

The King's Head Hotel

Much of this walk is along the edge of Bodmin Moor, with rolling hills stretching away in every direction. You reach it along a quiet, hedge-fringed lane that leads nowhere and return via farm fields and tracks. The views for most of the way are outstanding, but the route is mainly flat, even on the open moor.

Distance: *$4\frac{3}{4}$ miles*

OS Explorer 109 Bodmin Moor
GR 225807

An easy route, but with a 300 yard stretch in the middle that can become muddy, so go suitably shod

Starting point: The King's Head. The landlord has no objection to customers leaving their cars in the car park while they walk, but please ask first. There is also space in the road.

How to get there: The village is just off the A30, about 8 miles west of Launceston, and is clearly marked.

Built in 1623, the **King's Head Hotel**, a former coaching inn, had a chequered history in the Civil War, with burn marks dating from Roundhead attacks apparently still in the loft. These days it is a very welcoming hostelry. The main bar has a low, beamed ceiling and a large granite fireplace, and beyond it is a small restaurant with a slate floor and little windows. The public bar offers games, and there are some tables outside. The freshly-made food ranges from soup, ploughman's lunches and jacket potatoes to steak pie, scampi and steaks. There is a Sunday carvery, for which booking is recommended.

Telephone: 01566 86241.

The Walk

1 Cross the pub car park and at the end turn right (signposted to Bodmin). Continue along this road, ignoring the next sign for Bodmin, which points left. At the T-junction bear right along the road marked 'No access to the A30'. This leads you to the neighbouring village of Trewint; follow the road round to the left. The route follows the lane, which goes right in Trewint (signposted to Westmoorgate), but you might like to take a small detour to the left opposite it, to visit Wesley Cottage. This is a delightful little cottage, once owned by Digory Isbell, a local stonemason who gave John Wesley shelter and somewhere to preach when he first came to Cornwall. It is now owned by the Methodist Church and is a small museum with free entry (although there is a box for donations).

Follow the lane out of Trewint, and after 600 yards you will cross a cattle grid onto Trewint Downs, which are covered in common gorse, providing a mass of yellow in spring and early summer. There is a good view ahead of you to Bodmin Moor, and across to the right you can see the turbines of the wind farm on Napp's Moor. After another ½ mile you come to a gate and the end of the lane. *(1½ miles)*

2 Continue along the rough track on the other side. It gradually becomes less discernible and then swings left; as it does so, go straight on up the gentle hill ahead of you. As you come over the brow of that hill, you will see the steep slopes of Brown Willy, the highest point in Cornwall, on the horizon ahead of you. Pause to enjoy the stillness of the moor and the superb views all around you. Apart from the wind turbines on the right-hand horizon and a ruined farm in the distance half right, there is no sign of human habitation, just moorland rolling away into the distance in every direction. As you come down the hill on the other side, bear right and you will see a ford across a stream in the valley below; aim for that. *(¾ mile)*

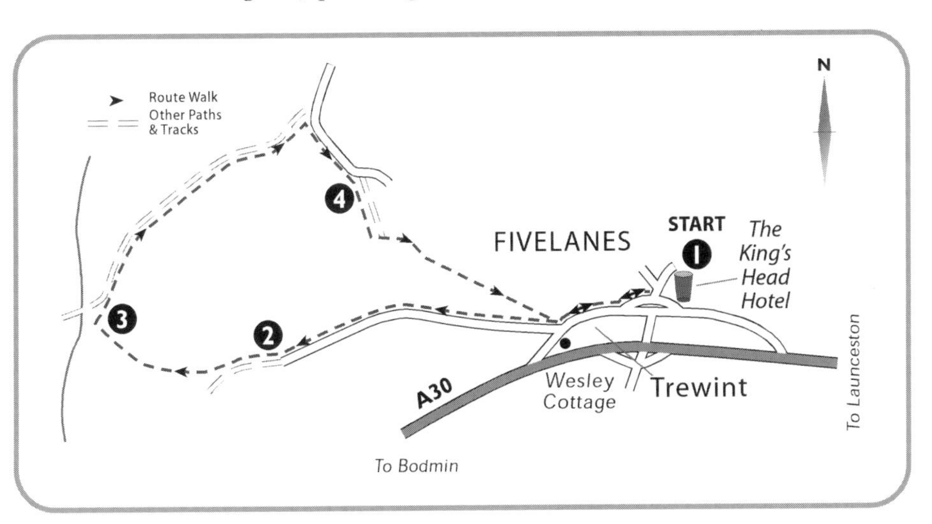

❸ When you reach the track that crosses the ford turn right, away from the stream, and follow the track round to the left. As you go you get another excellent view across the fields ahead of you. The track becomes somewhat indistinct, but as it does so you will see a wall ahead of you, with a very clear track running to the right of it. Aim for that and follow it, initially alongside the wall but then a little distance away from it. It takes you down off the moor to a gate and out onto a lane. Turn right and follow the lane for 1/4 mile past a farm. When it turns sharply to the left, go straight on along a track, following the public footpath sign. *(1 mile)*

❹ The track can become rather mucky at times with mud and slurry, but it is only about 300 yards long and is quite passable. Towards the end you will come to two gates on your left and a third a little further on straight ahead. Take the second gate on the left and follow another track to cross a stream. Instead of following it round to the right at the bottom, go straight on to a stile in the corner of the field. This leads to a path between banks, at the end of which are a small footbridge and another stile. Keep to the left of the narrow field on the other side to reach another stile over a wall.

Follow the right-hand boundary of the next field until you come to a gate. Go straight across another field to a stone stile across the wall ahead of you. Cross yet another field to another stone stile and keep to the left. At the end of this field is another stile and just beyond it a gate on the left; go through and turn right along the hedge, keeping it on your right. Go through a gate at the end and then diagonally right across the last field to another gate, which leads onto a lane. Turn left. You are now in Trewint and on the lane you took on the outward leg. At the T-junction in the centre of the village turn left and, after 1/4 mile, left again to return to Fivelanes and the pub. *(1 1/2 miles)*

Date walk completed:

....

Places of Interest Nearby

Wesley Cottage in Trewint, can be reached with a short detour from this route. Telephone 01566 86158. **Launceston,** 8 miles to the west, has a number of attractions, including the remains of the **Norman castle** (English Heritage), telephone: 01566 772365, and the **Launceston Steam Railway**. Telephone: 01566 775665.

Port Isaac 25 Walk

The Golden Lion

This is a spectacular stretch of the north Cornish coast: rugged cliffs, rocky coves and pretty fishing harbours. There are also views to take your breath away – but they come at a price, since the terrain is characterised not only by a constant series of inlets and bays but also by steep-sided valleys. Our route explores two of the most attractive harbours and the coast and countryside in between. The outward leg is along pretty farm paths and quiet lanes, while the return is along the rocky Coast Path.

The **Golden Lion**, over 500 years old, faces onto Port Isaac's harbour. A smugglers' tunnel, said to be frequented by the ghost of a drowned smuggler, runs underneath.

There are two bars, one with a spectacular view straight down the harbour, the other with an open fireplace. Outside is a lovely terrace and there is also a harbour patio. The cellar houses an atmospheric restaurant, open in the evenings during the summer. The bar food ranges from home-made crab soup, sandwiches and jacket potatoes to fish pie and a variety of daily specials. Unsurprisingly, fresh fish is a speciality, and it is all home-cooked.

Telephone: *01208 880336.*

Distance: ***6½ miles***

OS Explorer 106 Newquay and Padstow GR 996806 (pub) 999809 (car park)

A challenging walk; fairly easy on the outward leg, but with a lot of ascent and descent along the Coast Path on the way back

Starting point: The main pay and display car park at Port Isaac. The pub has no car park, and although there is parking in the harbour, the space is small and it is subject to the tides - it is only available when the tide is out.

How to get there: Turn north off the B3314 between Wadebridge and Delabole, onto the B3267. This takes you straight to Port Isaac, where the car park is clearly signposted. The Golden Lion is in the main street (more of a lane) through the old part of the village.

The Walk

1 Go down to the far left-hand corner of the car park as you face the sea; there you will find a track following the line of the coast. The views start straight away, as you can see all the way round Port Isaac Bay to your right. Follow the track round to the left and take the surfaced path going right, marked with the Coast Path sign. You go down some steps and swing left again. The path comes out onto a narrow lane; bear right, and at the T-junction go right again. Follow this lane down into the old village, which is a warren of tightly packed cottages, lanes and alleys. You pass the Golden Lion on your right and the lane swings right after it. Pass the harbour, also on your right and follow the lane round to the left. After another 100 yards or so you will come to a footpath sign on the left, pointing to Trewetha. *(½ mile)*

2 Turn off here and follow the path between hedges – it can become a little overgrown at times. Go through a gate and emerge into a field; keep to the right to reach a gate. Keep to the left of the next field to another gate, leading onto a drive. Follow the drive for a few yards, when you will find a gate on the left marked with a yellow footpath waymark. Go through and follow the path alongside a fence. At the junction, where a path goes left to Trewetha, go straight on. About 50 yards beyond the junction, look out for a path going sharp right; there is a post with a waymark, but no sign. Turn there and climb a hill, keeping alongside the bank on the left.

You come out onto a drive; go straight on. As you climb, you get a good view down onto Port Isaac. The drive swings left over a cattle grid and continues to climb. When it swings left again, go right across a stile and keep to the left of a field. At the end you will see another stile on the left, by a gate; cross it and turn right. You emerge onto a track. Pass a house and go through an archway in another, onto a lane. *(1 mile)*

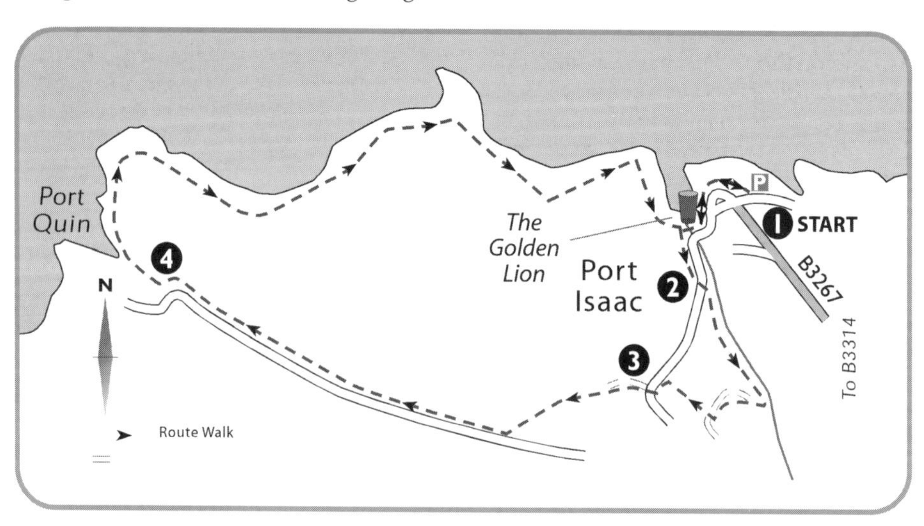

❸ Turn left, and after 100 yards, when the lane bends left, turn right along a smaller lane, following the public footpath sign. This takes you past some pretty cottages; where the lane ends go left, following the yellow waymark. Cross a couple of small streams then a stile. Keep to the left of the field on the other side and cross a stone stile into another field. Go straight across to a wooden stile, cross a track to another stone stile and go over the next field to yet another stone stile.

This leads into a peaceful and beautiful lane; turn right. The lane descends, gently at first and then more steeply, and after about a mile you come to the lovely little harbour of Port Quin. *(1½ miles)*

Port Quin

❹ At the bottom, just as the lane swings left to cross a stream, turn right, following the Coast Path sign. Climb some steps and then cross a stile. As you follow Port Quin harbour, you will see Doyden Castle on the other side. Built in 1830 as a businessman's retreat, it is more of a folly than a castle, and is now let by the National Trust as holiday accommodation. The path swings right round a little cove and then goes down some steps. It then swings right and climbs more steps, then right again, with yet more steps. At the top another lovely view opens up ahead of you around Port Isaac Bay and beyond – this view will stay with you for the rest of the walk.

The winding path continues for about 1½ miles and, as Port Isaac comes into view, cross a stile on the right to cut across Varley Head to another stile and continue along the coast on the other side. After ¾ mile you round another headland and find Port Isaac harbour on your left. Some steps lead down towards the harbour. Turn left and follow the lane up to the Golden Lion. To return to the car park, continue up, and where the lane swings right, go left, following the Coast Path sign, and follow the path round the cliff edge. *(3½ miles)*

Date walk completed:

....

Place of Interest Nearby

At Kilkhampton, about 4 miles north of Bude, there is **Brocklands Adventure Park**, with rides, an assault course, a soft play area and other children's attractions. Telephone: 01288 321920.

Walk 26 Wadebridge

The Molesworth Arms Hotel

The Camel Trail is a popular cycle and walking route along the disused railway line from Bodmin to Padstow. As its name suggests, it also follows the River Camel for much of its course. This beautiful walk, which will appeal particularly to flower lovers for much of the year, takes you along green lanes and through a wood to join the trail a couple of miles above Wadebridge. You then follow it back to town, with the chance to enjoy short detours to explore the flower-rich surroundings.

The **Molesworth Arms Hotel** is a beautiful 16th-century coaching inn, with an archway leading through from Molesworth Street. The low-beamed, characterful main bar contains two little snugs, each with a large stone fireplace. Leading off it is an attractive eating area. Beyond the archway is a patio bar with outdoor tables and flower baskets. There is also an elegant restaurant, open in the evenings. Given Wadebridge's proximity to the ports of Padstow and Port Isaac it is hardly surprising that seafood is a speciality. The bar menu is extremely varied, however, ranging from baguettes, burgers and ploughman's lunches to salads, steaks and vegetarian dishes.

Telephone: *01208 812055.*

Distance: *5¾ miles*

OS Explorer 106 Newquay and Padstow GR 989724 (pub) 990724 (car park)

An easy walk along clear tracks and paths, with just one gentle climb

Starting point: The Jubilee pay and display car park (the hotel car park is for residents only).

How to get there: Wadebridge is on the A39 south of Camelford, at the junction with the A389 to Bodmin. There are two main car parks in the town centre; the Jubilee one is on the south-eastern side of town, alongside the Co-op and the river, down a turning just beyond the tourist information office. The Molesworth Arms is in the pedestrianised Molesworth Street which stretches up from the river.

The Walk

❶ Go to the far right-hand corner of the car park as you face the river. Follow the surfaced path there through a park. When you come to a footbridge, turn right along another path alongside the river. This comes out by a road and follows it for a while. It joins the road at its end, near a sign for the Camel Trail. Cross the road and take a small lane that runs alongside it for a few yards. Where it forks, go left, following the public footpath sign, up a track. At the top is a stile; keep to the right of the field beyond, and at the end go through a gate onto a green lane. It is beautiful and tranquil here and the green lane is a haven for wild flowers in season.

You come out at a track; go straight on and just before you get to a house turn left along another track. After a few yards bear right at a fork and you come to another green lane. It climbs gently to a gate; go

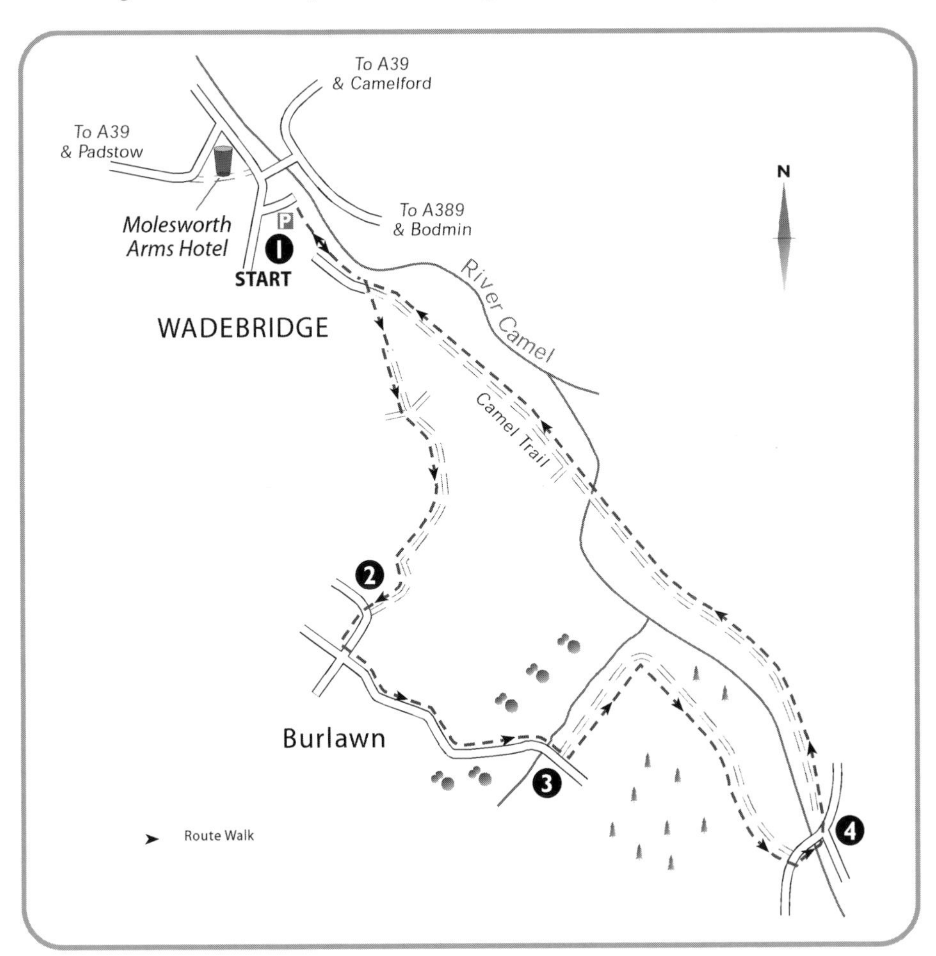

through and continue climbing. It is a long but not very steep hill. At the top, just before a gate into a field, the green lane swings left; follow it and again as it swings right. It emerges onto a lane. *(1½ miles)*

2 Go straight on along the lane, and at the crossroads 200 yards further on, turn left (signposted to Burlawn). Descend through Burlawn and, at the junction, follow the main lane round to the left and then to the right. It starts to descend quite steeply through a lovely wood and continues to curve to the left and right, and finally crosses a stream. Just beyond the stream is a public footpath sign pointing left; ignore it and continue for a few more yards to a forest track leading left. *(1 mile)*

3 Cross a stile next to a barrier and follow the track into a conifer wood. After 600 yards it turns right; follow it round. After a while you will see the River Camel through the trees on the left. You then leave the river for a while. Shortly afterwards, go past another barrier onto a lane and turn left to cross Polbrook Bridge. *(1 mile)*

4 Just before a second bridge, turn left down some steps and join the broad track that is the Camel Trail; turn left. As you join the trail, there is the opportunity to take a diversion to the left into an attractive unimproved water meadow.

After about a mile the trail crosses the river and then, after another ¾ mile, you come to a gate. Pass it and follow the last stretch of track to the road and path you came out on. Where the path goes right along the river, follow it. At the footbridge turn left to return to the car park. For the hotel, go through the car park and past the Co-op, and turn left at the roundabout, up Molesworth Street. *(2¼ miles)*

A sculpture along the Camel Trail

Date walk completed:

Places of Interest Nearby

About 4 miles south-east of Wadebridge, just off the A389, is the Georgian **Pencarrow House**. Telephone: 01208 841369. Five miles to the south-west, off the A39, is **Crealy Adventure Park**. Telephone: 01841 541215.

St Neot 27

The London Inn

This lovely route provides a rich variety of scenery. It combines a pretty village, deserted lanes fringed with hedges and wild flowers in summer, breathtaking views, shady woods and tumbling streams. There is also a saint's well you can visit along the way, and the St Neot Stone, the remnants of a 10th-century holed cross, along with some interesting wayside crosses, in the churchyard next to the pub. The granite church itself is also worth a visit.

***Distance:** 4¾ miles*

OS Explorer 109 Bodmin Moor
GR 186679 (pub) 184678 (car park)

An easy walk along lanes and clear paths, with one fairly steep climb at the start and a short one in the middle

Starting point: The free car park at the western end of the village - the pub has only a forecourt for parking, so please do not park there while walking.

How to get there: Turn north off the A38 Bodmin to Liskeard road just west of Doublebois, or south off the A30 between Bodmin and Launceston. St Neot is clearly signposted from both roads.

The 17th century **London Inn** was originally a coaching house – strange as it may seem today, this quiet backwater was once on the main road from Bodmin to London. It comprises one large bar subdivided into interesting little alcoves and different eating and drinking areas and open fires in winter. A terrace in the front is a pleasant place to sit on fine days. The menu is wide ranging, from sandwiches, ciabatta and jacket potatoes to fish and steak dishes, and interesting specials such as sweet and sour chicken.

Telephone: 01579 320263.

The Walk

1 Turn right from the car park and cross the river. Immediately on the other side you will see a lane on your left; turn up it for a short detour of about 300 yards if you would like to see the well of St Neot (or more properly St Anietus), an 8th-century Celtic missionary. The London Inn is 100 yards further up on the left. Turn left just before it up a small lane and climb out of the village. After 250 yards the lane swings to the right; as it does so, turn left up another lane.

After a few yards, turn right up some steps, following the public footpath sign. Go through a gate and keep right on the other side. At the top go through the second gate on your right and follow a short path between hedges to some steps and another gate. Walk straight across the next field. Cross a stone stile on the other side into a lane and turn left. After 50 yards you come to a T-junction; turn right. After 3/4 mile you come to another T-junction. *(1 1/4 miles)*

2 Walk straight across into a green lane, following the public bridleway sign. Go through a gate and onto Berry Down. Follow the line of waymarked stakes indicating the path. On your right you will see Berry Castle, a prehistoric settlement. On the other side of the

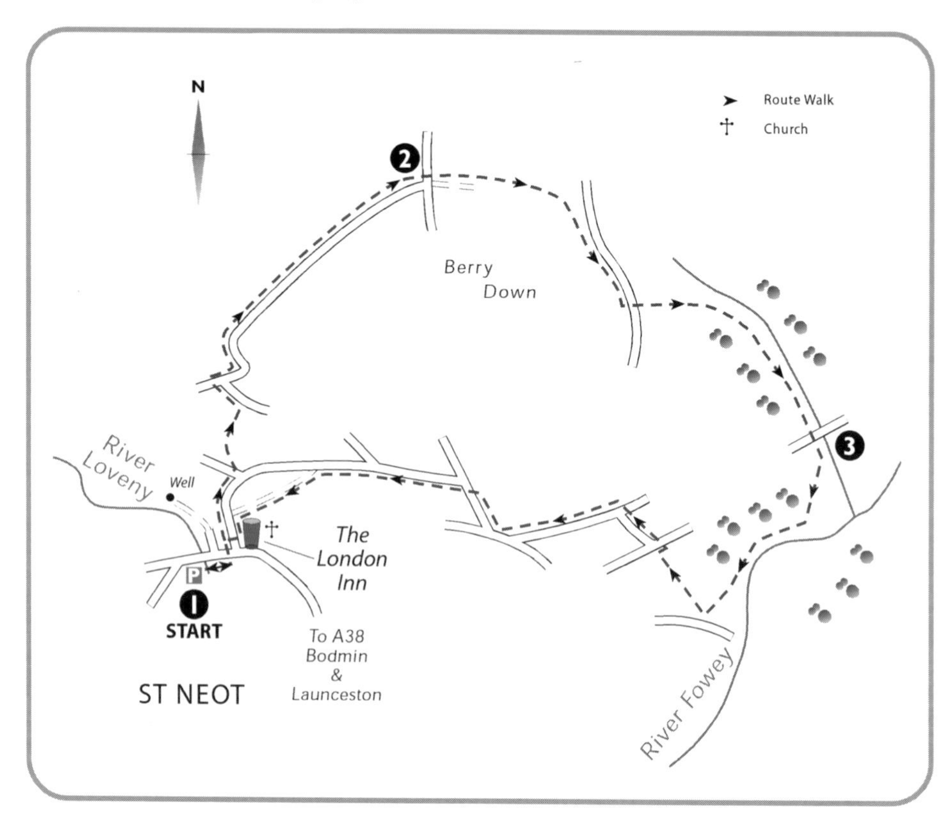

Near St Neot

down, go through another gate onto a lane; turn right. After 1/4 mile, just beyond a house called Higher Bowden, you will see a footpath on the left; follow it into a small wood.

At the end a stile takes you into a field. Bear left and go through a gateway. Head down the next field to another gateway. Cross the next field to a stile leading into a pretty mixed wood. Follow the path on the other side down through the trees, and soon you will see a river cascading below you on your left. The path eventually joins another one; bear left and follow the new path, which ends at a gate almost 1/2 mile after you entered the wood. Cross a field to another gate, which leads into a lane. *(1 1/4 miles)*

❸ Turn left and then immediately right along a track, following the public footpath sign. At the end, cross a stile and bear right to a gateway leading into another wood. Cross a stile and follow the path alongside the river. This is another lovely woodland stretch, with the river tumbling bedside you. You walk through a small field and about 1/4 mile after joining the river you cross a stile and climb some steps away from it. Go over another stile and then almost immediately another one on your right, into a field. Bear right up the field to another stile and then bear left to the corner of a wall. Go round it to a gate to a lane.

Cross to another lane and follow it through some trees to a T-junction; turn left. After 500 yards you come to a junction; bear right (signposted to St Neot) and, at the crossroads a short distance further on, turn right (signposted to Colliford Lake). After another 200 yards you will come to another junction; turn left. As you reach the brow of a rise you get another lovely view to your left and ahead. At the fork, follow the main lane to the left. After 300 yards follow the green lane on your left, opposite a farm. It leads you between high banks, with the trees forming a arch above you, and comes out at the surfaced lane you went out on. At the bottom you will find the pub on your left; turn right to return to the car park. *(2 1/4 miles)*

Date walk completed:

Places of Interest Nearby
Carnglaze Caverns. A disused slate quarry is 1 mile down the road towards the A38. Telephone: 01579 320251. Four miles away, just off the A38 at Dobwalls, is the **Dobwalls Family Adventure Park.** Telephone: 01579 320325.

Walk 28 St Dominick

The Who'd Have Thought It

Woods and river views are the main features of this lovely route. It follows lanes down to the National Trust's Cotehele estate, with a view across the Tamar River to the rolling farmland of Devon on the other side. At Cotehele Quay, with its museum of maritime history, it leaves the road and follows tracks and paths through the delightful woodland of the estate, with more superb views up the Tamar. It then climbs across fields and returns to St Dominick along lanes and green lanes, with yet more farmland views.

Distance: *5 miles*

OS Explorer 108 Lower Tamar Valley and Plymouth
GR 407674

A moderate walk along lanes and easy paths, but with a couple of stiff climbs in the middle

Starting point: The Who'd Have Thought It. The landlord has no objection to customers leaving their cars there while walking, as long as they ask. Alternatively, there is street parking in St Dominick itself, about ½ mile away. If you park in the village, you should start the walk towards the end of point 4.

How to get there: Turn east off the A388 Launceston to Saltash road between Callington and St Mellion, and follow the signs for St Dominick. At the T-junction at the entrance to the village, turn right for the pub, left for the village centre. If you are parking in the village, take the second turning right after the T-junction and you will find parking spaces down that road.

The 19th-century, stone-walled **Who'd Have Thought It** inn got its strange name from a previous landlord, who gave up a career in London to become a Cornish innkeeper. His friends' reaction, 'Who'd have thought he would do that?', renamed the pub. There are three bars, two with open fireplaces and one with games, and a large, comfortable lounge. At the back there is a light, airy conservatory and a small garden, both with excellent river views. The menu includes light snacks such as soup and scampi and mouthwatering main dishes like poached salmon and chicken balti.

Telephone: *01579 350214.*

The Walk

❶ Turn right out of the pub car park and follow the lane as it heads gently down towards the valley, passing first a lane going to the right, the next to the left. You go through the hamlet of Bohetherick, and soon you will be able to see the Tamar River below you. You pass a fruit farm on the right. The lane then swings left and runs parallel to the river and above it.

It descends into a wood. Soon you will see three deep holes fenced off on your right; these are the chimneys of limekilns on the riverbank. Just beyond them is a junction; turn right (signposted to Cotehele House). Cross a bridge and follow the lane to the right. The fronts of the limekilns can be seen on your right. The lane then bends to the left and you will see Cotehele Quay ahead of you. *(1½ miles)*

❷ Leave the lane here and cross the quay where you will see the Shamrock, a 19th-century barge, the last to ply the Tamar. There is also a National Trust tearoom offering refreshments. Go to the left of a car park on the other side of the quay to join a track and bear right. If you want to visit Cotehele House and garden, follow the path to the left. The main route continues along the edge of the wood.

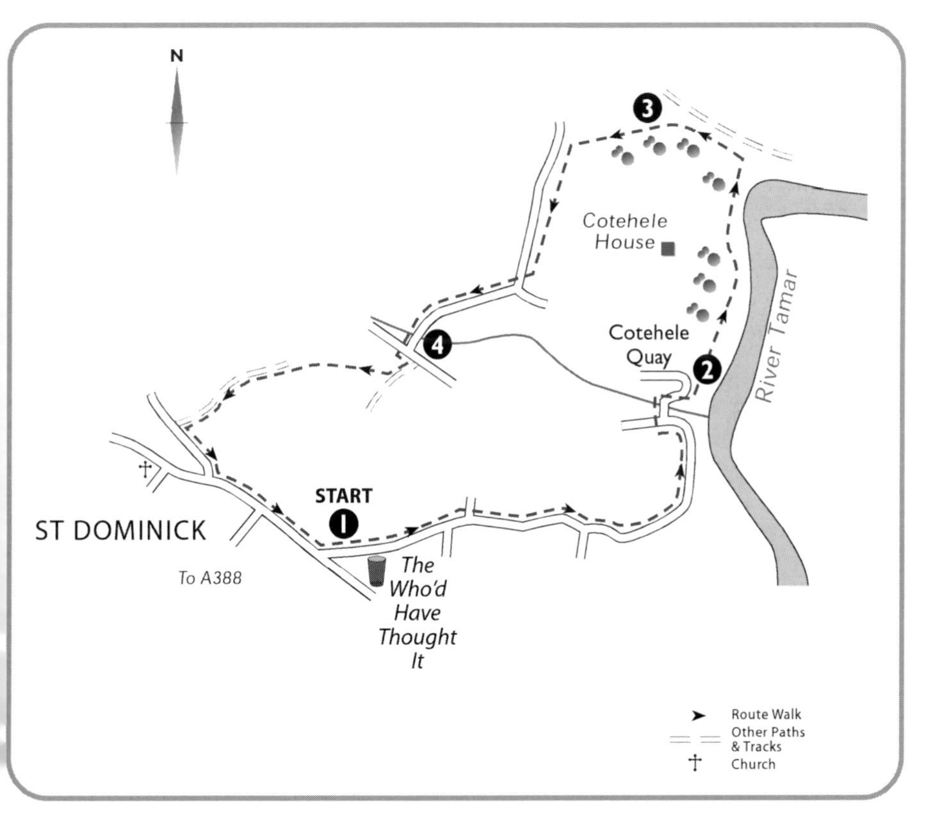

The Shamrock, a 19th-century Tamar barge

After just over $^1/_4$ mile you pass a 15th-century chapel and the track swings left and then right, climbing as it does so. You pass another path leading to the house and gardens, then come to a fork; keep to the main track, which soon descends through the trees. At the bottom turn left at T-junction along a track alongside a stream. *(1 mile)*

❸ After about 200 yards follow the path going left into the wood. It soon swings to the left and climbs straight up the hill. It is a steep ascent, but the surrounding woodland is lovely. You come to a track; turn right and after a few yards left to cross a stile into a field. Bear right across the field, aiming for the far right-hand corner; you will see a folly in the form of a tower in the field on your left. Cross a stile and keep to the right of the next field. Cross another stile at the end into a lane and turn left. At the junction after 600 yards follow the main lane round to the right (signposted to St Dominick, Harrowbarrow and Callington). You descend steeply, cross a bridge and come out at a T-junction. *(1 mile)*

❹ Turn left and almost immediately right up a sunken green lane into another wood. After about 200 yards you will see a public footpath sign pointing right. Turn off here and cross a stile into a field. As you cross this field, bearing slightly left, look back for a panoramic view. In the far corner there is another stile; cross it and keep left across the next field. Another good view appears on the right. A third stile takes you onto a track; bear right. After a while this track swings right to pass a farm and comes to the outskirts of St Dominick. At the T-junction go left; this is the road along which you may have left your car if you parked in the village. At the T-junction at the end turn left again, and follow the lane out of the village. After $^1/_2$ mile you will come to the pub. *($1^1/_2$ miles)*

Date walk completed:

Place of Interest Nearby
The 15th-century granite and slate National Trust house at **Cotehele**. Telephone: 01579 351346.

Lanlivery

The Crown Inn

This pretty, peaceful walk explores the two branches of the Saints' Way, a long-distance path that stretches from Padstow to Fowey, connecting a number of shrines, wells and other places holy to the early Celtic church. In the process it visits two delightful villages, tiny Lanlivery and larger Luxulyan, an attractive nature reserve and the imposing rock formation of Helman Tor.

Distance: *$6\frac{3}{4}$ miles*

OS Explorer 107 St Austell and Liskeard GR 079590

A moderate walk with few hills; one stretch can become muddy after rain, so go suitably shod

Starting point: The Crown Inn. The landlord is generally happy for customers to leave their cars in the pub car park, but please ask first.

How to get there: Turn north-west off the A390 Liskeard to St Austell road just south of Lostwithiel, and follow the signs for Lanlivery. The pub is in the centre of the village, opposite the church.

Parts of the beautifully preserved **Crown Inn** date back to the 12th century, when it accommodated the stonemasons working on the church opposite. The entrance is through the snug, slate-floored bar, which has an enormous granite fireplace with an old oven alongside. There is also a restaurant, with another large granite fireplace, and a light, plant-filled sunroom. The delightful beer garden has several shade-giving trees. Food ranges from baguettes and baked potatoes to pasties, salads and main courses.

Telephone: *01208 872707.*

The Walk

❶ Go through the beer garden to the end furthest from the car park and turn right onto a path. Follow it down to a stone stile. Bear left on the other side. Another stone stile takes you onto a concrete track to a farm. Go through two gates and follow the track on the other side round to the left. At the top, go left through a gateway and then bear right to follow the right-hand edge of the field beyond. Go through a gate at the end and keep to the right of the next field. Soon the spoil tips of the china clay works that are a feature of this part of Cornwall come into view ahead. At the end of the field cross a stile onto a track, which takes you to a lane. *(3/4 mile)*

❷ Bear left. After 250 yards you will find a lane going off to the left; go straight on. At the junction at the bottom, follow the main lane round to the right and cross a

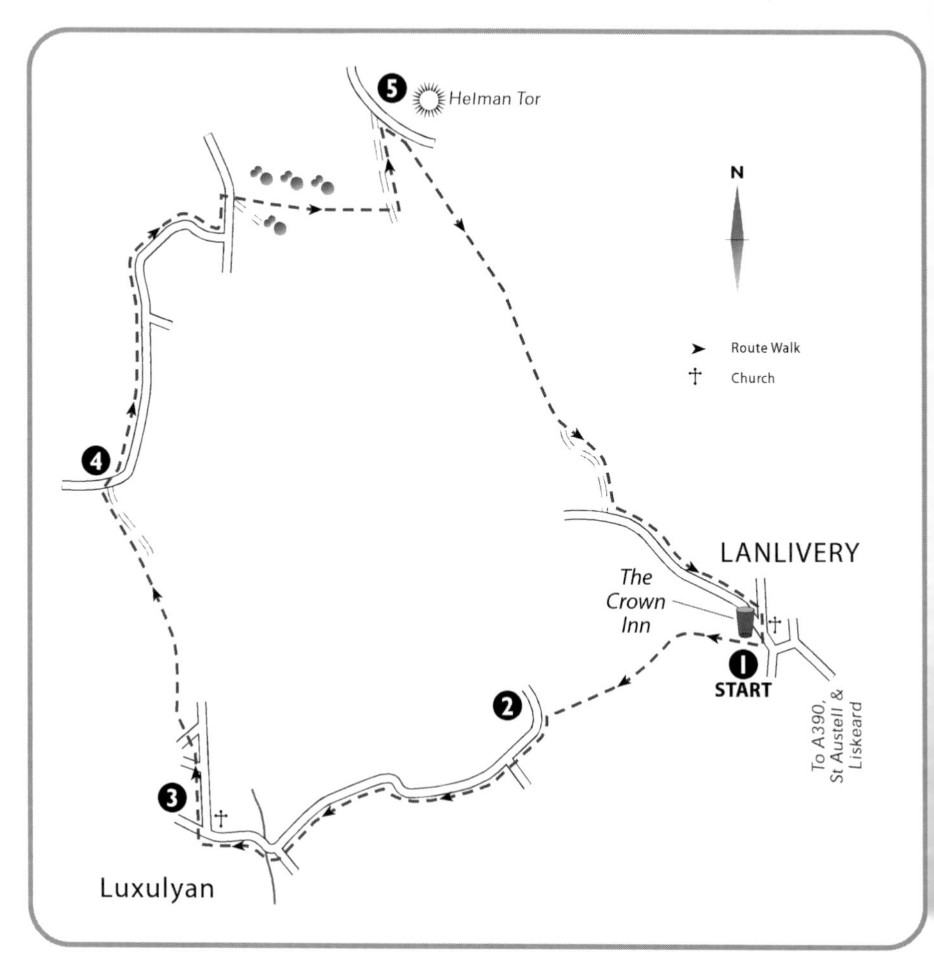

stream. Climb up the other side to the pretty village of Luxulyan. *(1¼ miles)*

3 Just beyond the church, turn right along another lane, marked with the Celtic cross waymark of the Saints' Way. At the junction go straight on, following the Saints' Way sign. Immediately after the de-restriction sign, take the path on the left indicated by the Saints' Way sign. Cross a lane after a few yards and then go over a stile into a field. Bear right and keep to the right of the field – do not follow the clear path straight across. Luxulyan Quarry is now close by on the right. You will come to a stile; cross it into a wood. Cross a footbridge and follow the path to the right.

Cross a stone stile; the next stretch can become muddy after rain. You cross another stone stile, followed by several small footbridges. The path then swings left to run alongside a small stream. Cross several more small footbridges and then swing right to cross a third stone stile. More little footbridges follow, and you finally emerge into a field. Keep to the left and at the end cross a stile to a boardwalk and another field. Keep to the left again and go through a gap in a fence. Cut diagonally right across the next field, aiming for the far right-hand corner. Cross a stile and go up to a track; turn left and go through a gate. *(1 mile)*

4 At the lane, turn right, following the Saints' Way sign. Helman Tor can be seen half right. After ½ mile you pass a farm and a junction; go straight on. The lane finally comes out at a T-junction; turn left. After 150 yards, just opposite some holiday cottages, turn right on a track into a wood. After a short distance you go through a kissing-gate into the Breney Common Nature Reserve. This is a very attractive area of woodland and wetland. Where the path forks at an information board beside a pretty pond, go right and through a gate. Two more gates follow, and after the last one the track becomes a path. You leave the nature reserve via a gateway and the path swings to the left and begins to climb. It comes out at a track; turn left. After ¼ mile you go through a gate and come out onto a road just below Helman Tor. *(1¾ miles)*

5 Turn right and follow the road as it climbs towards the tor. You are now on the other branch of the Saints' Way. When the road ends at a car park, you can turn left for a short detour to Helman Tor itself; otherwise continue along the path. After 500 yards you pass a public footpath sign on the right; go straight on. The path runs between banks and hedges along a ridge for about 1 mile. Bear right through a gate onto a track; the tower of Lanlivery church is ahead. The track comes out at a lane; turn left, again following the Saints' Way sign. At the crossroads, go straight on (signposted to Lanlivery). After another 500 yards or so you come to the village, with the Crown Inn on the right. *(2 miles)*

Date walk completed:

....

Places of Interest Nearby

Four miles north of Lanlivery is **Lanhydrock** (National Trust). Telephone: 01208 265950. Five miles to the south is the **Eden Project**. Telephone: 01726 811911.

Walk 30 Duloe

Ye Olde Plough House Inn

This is a pretty woodland ramble, with some delightful riverside stretches and one or two excellent views. It follows the West Looe River upstream to the attractive hamlet of Herodsfoot and then crosses to follow it downstream on the opposite bank. You then climb out of the valley to return to Duloe, with the chance to visit an interesting stone circle on the way.

Distance: *6¼ miles*

OS Explorer 107 St Austell and Liskeard GR 234585 (pub) 234584 (car park)

A moderate walk, mainly along forest tracks but with three steep (but not too long) climbs and one ford to negotiate

Starting point: The free public car park in the centre of Duloe. Please park there rather than in the pub car park.

How to get there: Duloe is on the B3254 Liskeard to Looe road. There is no direct access to this road from the Liskeard by-pass, so if you are on the A38 you should turn south at Dobwalls, following the sign for Duloe.

The atmospheric stone-built **Ye Olde Plough House Inn** comprises a large lounge and a smaller bar, both with slate floors covered with rugs, and both with large stone fireplaces housing wood-burning stoves. Behind the lounge is another very pleasant room, and there are tables on the grass outside. The food is excellent – indeed, it is best to book for evening eating, as the pub quickly fills. The speciality is steak cooked on hot stones (evening only), and the fish dishes are also good. The menu is wide ranging, from soup and snacks to lamb, chicken and specials such as pan-fried langoustine.

Telephone: *01503 262050.*

The Walk

❶ Turn left from the car park, and then almost immediately right down Tremadart Lane. This takes you out of the village, then swings right and descends between high banks into the valley of the West Looe River. It enters a wood, and near the bottom of the hill you will see another lane going off to the right. Turn along it and pass some cottages. You will find the river down below you on the left. The lane swings to the right and starts to climb. You pass a house on the left. A little way beyond it you will see a track on the left, with a public bridleway sign; take it. *(1¼ miles)*

❷ After about 100 yards you will see a path leading off to the left; follow that and you will soon find yourself on a broad path, with the river below you on the left. This is a lovely stretch of mixed deciduous and coniferous woodland.

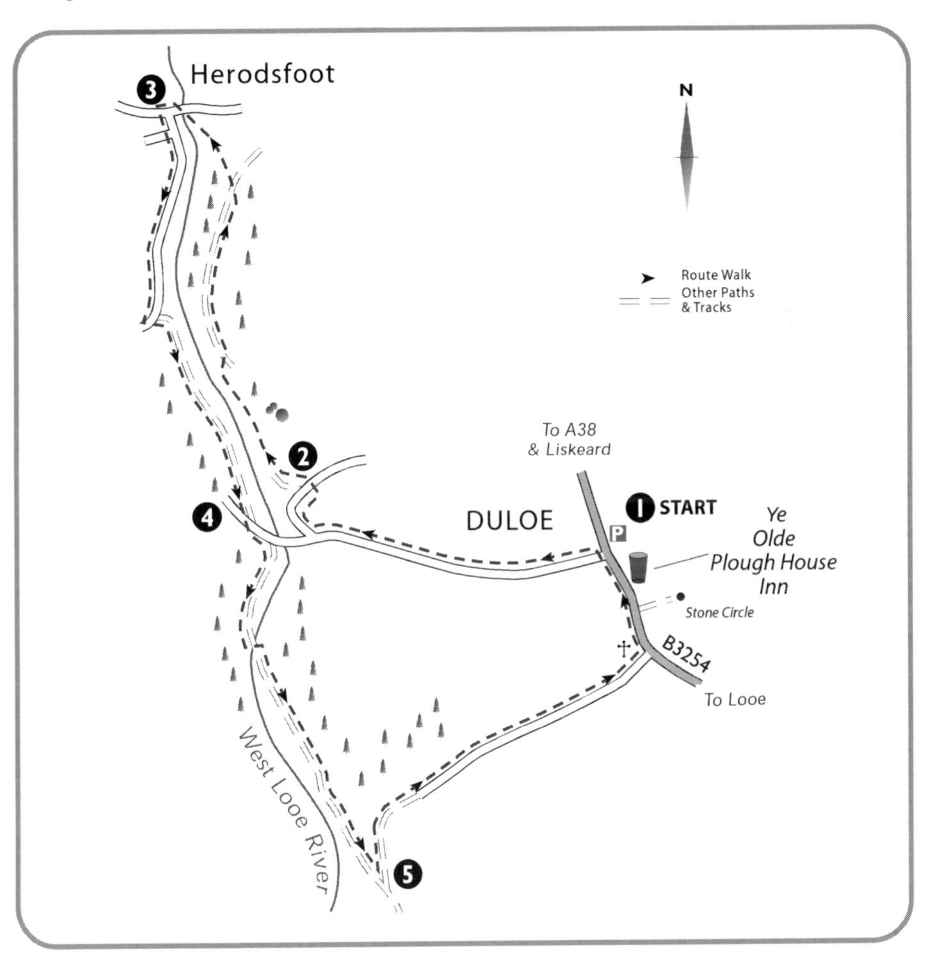

After 600 yards or so, the path swings left to cross a footbridge. Instead of following it, turn right up another path, which climbs steeply for a short distance to a track. Turn left and follow the track through the trees, which are now almost exclusively conifers. After about 1/2 mile you will come to a path crossing the track, with a post marked with different waymarks. Turn left and follow the path steeply down through the trees. You leave the wood and join the drive of a house; follow that past the house and continue past more houses to a lane in the centre of Herodsfoot. *(1 1/4 miles)*

3 Turn left and cross a bridge. On the other side turn left down a side lane. After a little over 1/2 mile you will find a forest road on the left, leading into Pendruffle Wood. Follow it round to the right. You can hear the river down on your left, and soon join it. You pass a bridge, but carry straight on along the track. A little over 1/2 mile after entering the wood you leave it again, emerging into a lane. *(1 1/4 miles)*

4 Turn left, and then, as the lane swings left across a bridge, go straight ahead onto another forest track. You will find this stretch ablaze with rosebay willowherb in late summer. After 500 yards you come to a gateway ahead of you; bear left to cross the river, following the blue waymark. There is a ford here and the crossing is fairly easy, but unless the river is very low you will have to get your feet wet. Climb the bank on the other side to a track and bear right. The rosebay willowherb is especially fine along here. About 600 yards after the crossing the track swings sharp left; when it does so go right across a V-stile and along a less distinct track. At the T-junction turn left and follow another track for 1/4 mile to a junction with another track, which goes sharp left. *(1 mile)*

5 Turn left and follow the new track as it climbs steeply out of the wood. At the top it becomes a surfaced lane. As you follow this lane you get excellent views through the gateways on your left and right, across the rolling farmland. After 3/4 mile you reach the outskirts of Duloe and soon come to a T-junction, with the attractive steepled church on your left. Turn left. After 150 yards you will come to a farm track on the right; you can turn up here for a short detour to visit a well-preserved prehistoric stone circle. Another 200 yards further on is Ye Olde Plough House Inn, and the car park is about 150 yards beyond that. *(1 1/2 miles)*

Date walk completed:

Places of Interest Nearby

In Dobwalls, 5 miles to the north of Duloe is the **Dobwalls Family Adventure Park**. Telephone: 01579 320325. About 3 miles away, on the Liskeard road, is **Paul Corin's Magnificent Music Machines**, a superb collection of organs, pianolas and player pianos. Telephone: 01579 343108.

The Rashleigh Inn

Variety is the keynote of this walk. From the pretty little hamlet of Polkerris you take the Saints' Way, a long-distance path that crosses Cornwall, linking various shrines and holy wells. This takes you across farms and through woods to the historic port of Fowey, with its steep, narrow lanes, traditional buildings and beautiful harbour. The return leg is along the South West Coast Path, and offers stunning views in both directions, as well as delightful coves and beaches.

Distance: *6¼ miles*

OS Explorer 107 St Austell and Liskeard GR 093521

A moderately challenging walk; the route follows easy paths and lanes, but it is somewhat hilly and there are some steep climbs

Starting point: Rashleigh Inn. Lunch customers may leave their cars in the car park while walking, but please ask first. Note that the car park is closed when the pub is closed. There is also a public car park at the top of the village, on the way in.

How to get there: Turn south off the A3082 St Austell to Fowey road and follow the signs for Polkerris.

The **Rashleigh Inn**, once a coastguard house, is a charming old building, right on the beach and with a terrace overlooking the sea. There is a comfortable bar, full of character, with dark panelled walls and a big bay window. Beyond is a stone-walled restaurant, light and airy, and also overlooking the water. The pub is open all day and there is a superb range of food, including fresh, locally caught fish and other local produce. In addition to light snacks such as ploughman's lunches and sandwiches, there are also steaks, pies and vegetarian offerings and various daily specials like lobster thermidor and game pie.

Telephone: *01726 813991.*

The Walk

❶ Turn left from the pub, and after a few yards turn right up a lane, following the sign for the toilets. At the end of the lane take the path into a wood. At the junction turn right, following the yellow waymark with the Coast Path acorn. The path climbs some steps and zigzags fairly steeply up through the wood, emerging into a field. At the next junction, where the Coast Path goes right, go straight on across a field. At the end go through a gate into a lane, and turn right. After about 100 yards you will come to a track on the left, leading to Tregaminion, with a Saints' Way sign on the right; turn down it. At the end of the track turn right. After a few yards, just before you get to the main farm buildings, you will see a yellow waymark on a wall on the right, pointing left. Turn left down a small track and at the bottom you will see two gates; go through the one on the left and cross the field beyond to a stone stile. Bear right on the other side to skirt

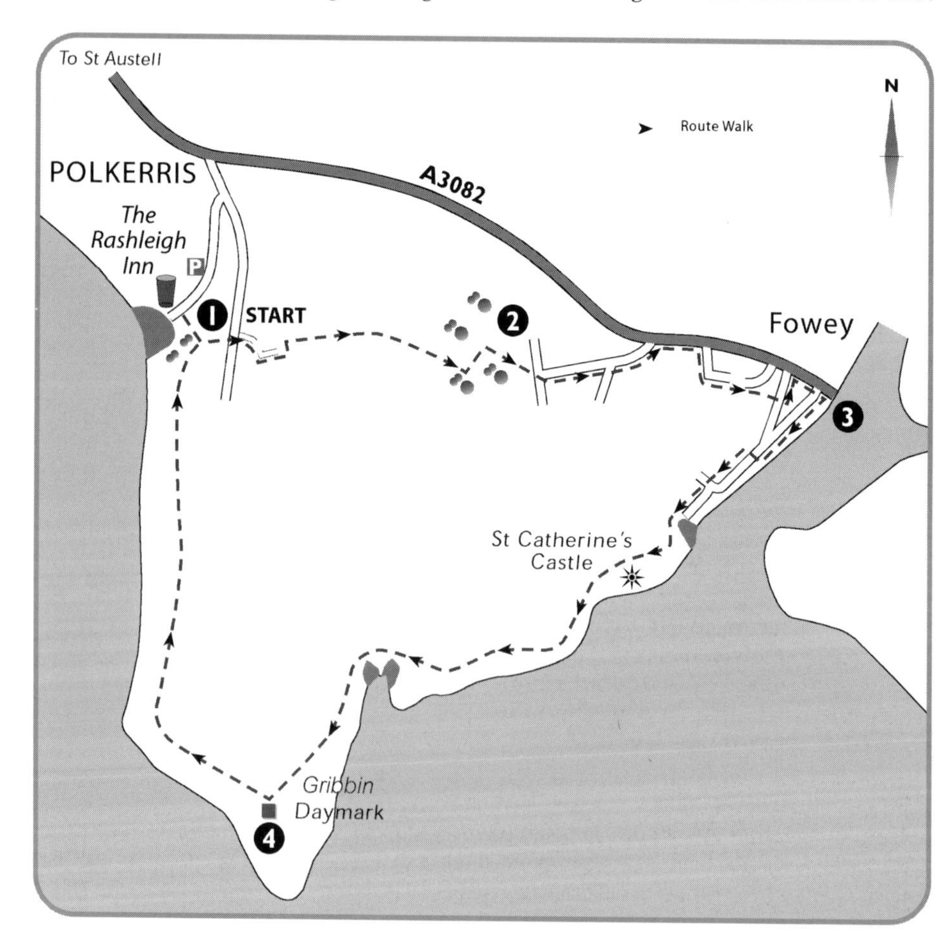

a field and at the end cross a small footbridge and climb the hill beyond it.

Go through a gate at the top and keep to the right of the next field. At the end cross a stone stile onto a surfaced drive; go over it to a wooden stile and continue between a hedge and a fence. After about 600 yards cross another stone stile and enter a small wood. The path swings to the left and crosses a stile and a small stream before swinging right again. Go through a gate and follow the path alongside a house to a lane. *(1¼ miles)*

2 Turn right and almost immediately left down Lankelly Lane. At the roundabout turn right for ¼ mile to another roundabout; turn right again down Windmill. Follow the road round to the left, and where it ends go straight on across a car park to follow the road on the other side. When it turns left, go straight on down a path and some steps. At the road, go straight across, down Daglands Hill which ends at another little lane; turn right and follow it down to the harbour. *(1 mile)*

3 To resume the walk, go back up the hill for about 100 yards and turn left along Esplanade. Follow it above the river, and at the T-junction go straight on. At the next junction, go straight on along Readymoney Road. When it ends, go straight on along a surfaced path. It climbs to a junction; go left, following the acorn Coast Path waymark. The path climbs up through a wood. At the next junction go straight on to find St Catherine's Castle on the left.

Follow the path as it goes inland for a bit; at the T-junction go left and through a gate into Allday's Fields. At the end cross a stile and go down and above the beach at Coombe Haven. Climb up the other side of the valley and go through a gate. Keep to the left of a field. At the end cross the stile on the right and then a small footbridge and go left. Follow the coast round to the right and go through a gate. You then walk to the left and cross a stream above a beach, with a lawn and lake on the right. Follow the path round to the left on the other side and turn left at a junction. Go through a gate and climb a fairly steep hill. At the top you will find the Gribbin daymark, a large tower built as a navigation aid. *(2½ miles)*

4 Continue past the daymark, bearing right to a gate. Follow the path on the other side. The path joins a track; bear left and when the track ends at a gate go round the path to the left. Cross a stile and go through a gate. Go through another gate at the end of the field and skirt the edge of a field, to yet another gate. The path now runs between two banks, and comes out at a broad path. Turn sharp left into the wood to join the path on which you came out. Follow it and when you reach the green lane at the end turn left and then right. At the end of the lane beyond some toilets, turn right for the car park or left for the Rashleigh Inn. *(1½ miles)*

Date walk completed:

....

Place of Interest Nearby

About 6 miles west of Polkerris, on the outskirts of St Austell, is the **Charlestown Shipwreck Rescue and Heritage Centre**, where there are displays of artefacts from shipwrecks, as well as sections on village life and Cornish mining (telephone 01726 69897).

Walk 32 Cawsand

The Cross Keys Inn

This stretch of the Cornish coast is quite beautiful, punctuated as it is by small coves and pretty villages. One such village is Cawsand, a delightful collection of narrow streets and alleys and slate-roofed cottages, which is worth exploring at the end of your walk. Our route is extremely varied, with superb coastal and farmland views, lanes that are full of flowers for much of the year, interesting sights and a pretty wood to finish with.

Distance: *5¼ miles*

OS Explorer 108 Lower Tamar Valley and Plymouth
GR 434502 (pub) 432503 (car park)

A short but fairly challenging walk, with some steep climbs, including one right at the start

Starting point: The pay and display car park just to the west of Cawsand. There is no parking in the centre of the village.

How to get there: Take the B3247 south off the A374 Liskeard to Torpoint road and turn right about ½ mile beyond Millbrook, following the signs for Kingsand and Cawsand. Follow the road above the two villages and you will see the Cawsand car park on the left.

The delightful little **Cross Keys Inn** is situated right in the centre of this pretty fishing village. The bar has dark beams and a bare wooden floor, while the raised eating area is carpeted and furnished with pine tables and chairs. Old photographs of the area decorate the walls throughout. Alternatively, if the weather is fine, you can sit at tables and benches laid out in front, in the village square itself. As one would expect, fresh fish is a speciality, but various sandwiches are offered, also jacket potatoes, soups and a range of main courses, including daily specials such as grilled local lamb.

Telephone: *01752 822706.*

The Walk

❶ Leave the car park via the pedestrian exit at the village end and follow the road down into The Square; the Cross Keys Inn is on the left. Turn immediately left just after the pub and immediately left again into St Andrew's Street. At the top, where it joins the main road, cross over to a path and go through a kissing-gate. Follow the path on the other side between hedges to a stile leading into a field. Look back for a lovely view over Cawsand Bay. Go straight across to another kissing-gate, which leads into a lane.

Cross to a drive. Where it forks, go right and then turn immediately right again, following the public footpath sign. This takes you into a green lane; at the top go through a kissing-gate. Cross the field beyond to a gap in the hedge and

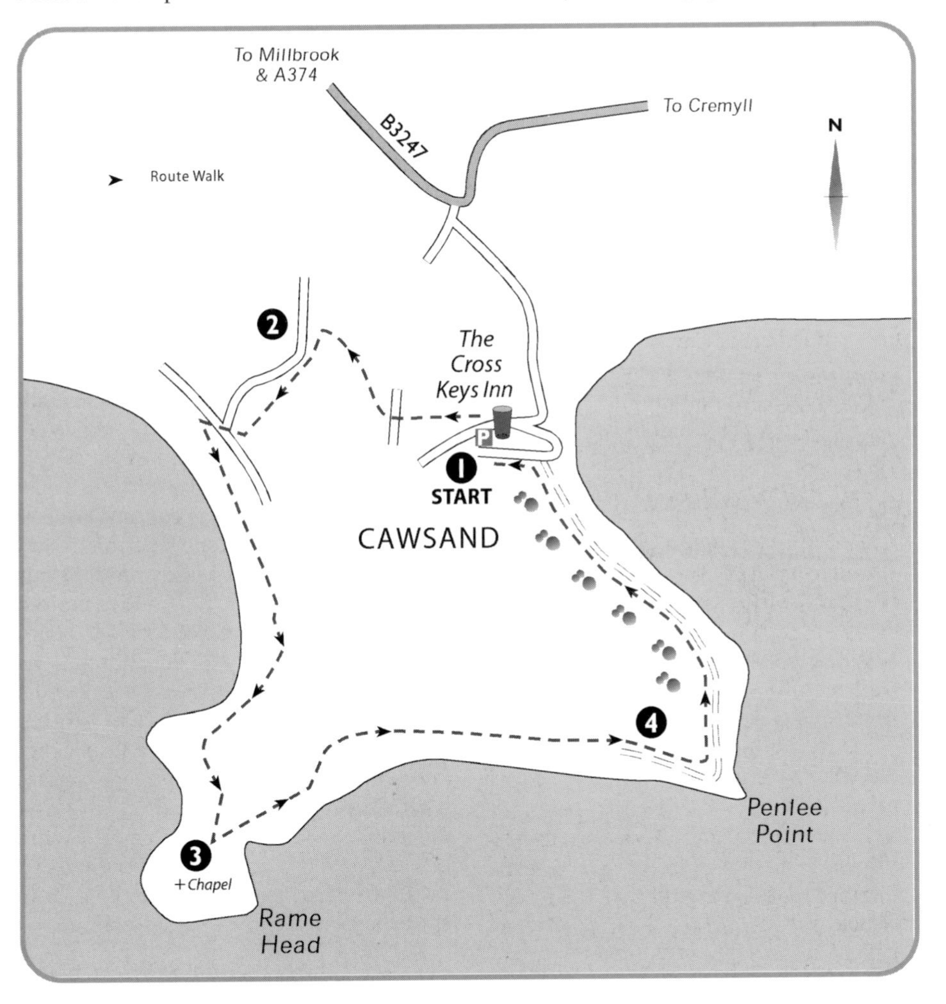

bear left along another green lane. This curves left past a house and emerges onto a lane. *(3/4 mile)*

❷ Bear left. The banks alongside the lane are a mass of flowers in the summer. You soon get another superb view out to sea ahead of you. The lane emerges at a car park; just before you reach it turn right and cross a main road to a track, following the Coast Path sign. Bear left along a path (signposted to Rame Head). It takes you down some steps and then swings left to follow the line of the coast. There is a wide variety of flowers alongside the path in season, and the slope on your right can be covered in yellow gorse. You pass a blockhouse and go through a kissing-gate. After a while you go through another kissing-gate onto a track. Turn right and just before a house turn left along a path.

As you follow this path you can see Polhawn Fort ahead of you. Built in the 1860s, this formed part of the defences of Plymouth. You climb some steps to the fort's drive; cross over and climb some more steps. At the top the path swings right and levels off. You then go through two kissing-gates; if you look right as you go, you get a lovely view across Whitsand Bay. The path swings left and climbs some more steps. You can now see Rame Head, with its 14th-century chapel, ahead of you. You come to a T-junction; turn right, following the Coast Path sign for Cawsand. After 300 yards you come to another junction. You can take a short detour to visit the chapel, or turn sharp left to continue the walk. *(2 miles)*

❸ The view now changes, encompassing a different stretch of coast – across Plymouth Sound and into the South Hams. After about 1/2 mile you cross a stile and come to a junction. Go straight on (signposted to Penlee Point and Cawsand). After another 3/4 mile you go through a kissing-gate onto a track. Walk straight on again. Where the track forks, go left, and follow it to Penlee Point. *(1 1/2 miles)*

❹ Here it swings sharp left into a beautiful, cool wood. After about 600 yards, when the surfaced track curves left, bear right along an unsurfaced track, following the Coast Path waymark. You emerge onto a lane; where that curves left, go straight on along a track, again following the Coast Path waymark. It emerges onto another lane, which again swings left after a few yards; go straight on along a surfaced path, again following the Coast Path waymark. You finally come out at a T-junction at the edge of Cawsand. Turn right and follow the road round to The Square, and the Cross Keys Inn is straight ahead of you. On the other hand, if you want to return to the car park, turn left at the T-junction. *(1 mile)*

Date walk completed:

....

Places of Interest Nearby

Mount Edgcumbe, a 15th-century house, garden and country park, is just 2 1/2 miles away to the north-east. Telephone: 01752 822236. Six miles away, near Torpoint, is the 18th-century **Antony House** (National Trust). Telephone: 01752 812191.

Portreath 33

The Basset Arms

This route is both spectacular and beautiful, combining a magnificent coastal stretch and a woodland amble, with a few farm paths and green lanes in between. You take the South West Coast Path along the beautiful cliff tops south-west of Portreath, with superb views along the coast, then head inland to join a track through the lovely mixed woods of Tehidy Country Park. A pretty, green lane brings you back to Portreath.

Distance: *$6\frac{1}{2}$ miles*

OS Explorer 104 Redruth and St Agnes GR 655452

A moderate walk overall, but with a couple of steep hills at the start

Starting point: The Basset Arms. The landlady has no objection to customers leaving their cars there while they walk, but do please ask first. Alternatively, there is a public car park about 50 yards along the road.

How to get there: Take the B3300 from Redruth. Follow it through Portreath to the beach, where it turns sharp left to climb out of the village. As it does so, you will see a small road going left; that leads to the Basset Arms.

The attractive **Basset Arms** is close to the beach and just opposite a pretty stream. The name derives from the local landowners, who lived at nearby Tehidy House. You enter through a light, airy conservatory, which leads into a comfortable L-shaped bar with dark beams and horse brasses, decorated with old photographs. Off the bar is the attractive restaurant. There is a terrace in the front, from which you can watch the world go by. The menu is wide ranging, from sandwiches, jacket potatoes and ploughman's lunches to steaks, fish dishes and daily specials such as chicken and sweetcorn pie.

Telephone: *01209 842077.*

The Walk

❶ Turn left as you leave the pub and walk to the main road; cross over to Battery Hill, following the Coast Path sign for Godrevy. You then round a promontory and go down a hill towards a small bay. The road ends at the bottom; bear left along a path (signposted as the North Coast Footpath). Go through a kissing-gate and straight on up a gentle gorse- and bracken-covered slope. You come to a T-junction by the edge of a cliff; turn left. Godrevy lighthouse is in the distance.

Go through a kissing-gate and bear right to follow the cliff round. The path soon swings sharply right and then left down a steep hill to go round an inlet. It then climbs steeply up the other side, zigzagging as it goes. It goes down some steps, crosses a wooden bridge and climbs up more steps on the other side. Once you reach the top, you can relax in the knowledge that there are no more major climbs to worry about. After another 1/4 mile you cross a stile and come to a car park. Cross it and follow the path to a kissing-gate. After following the

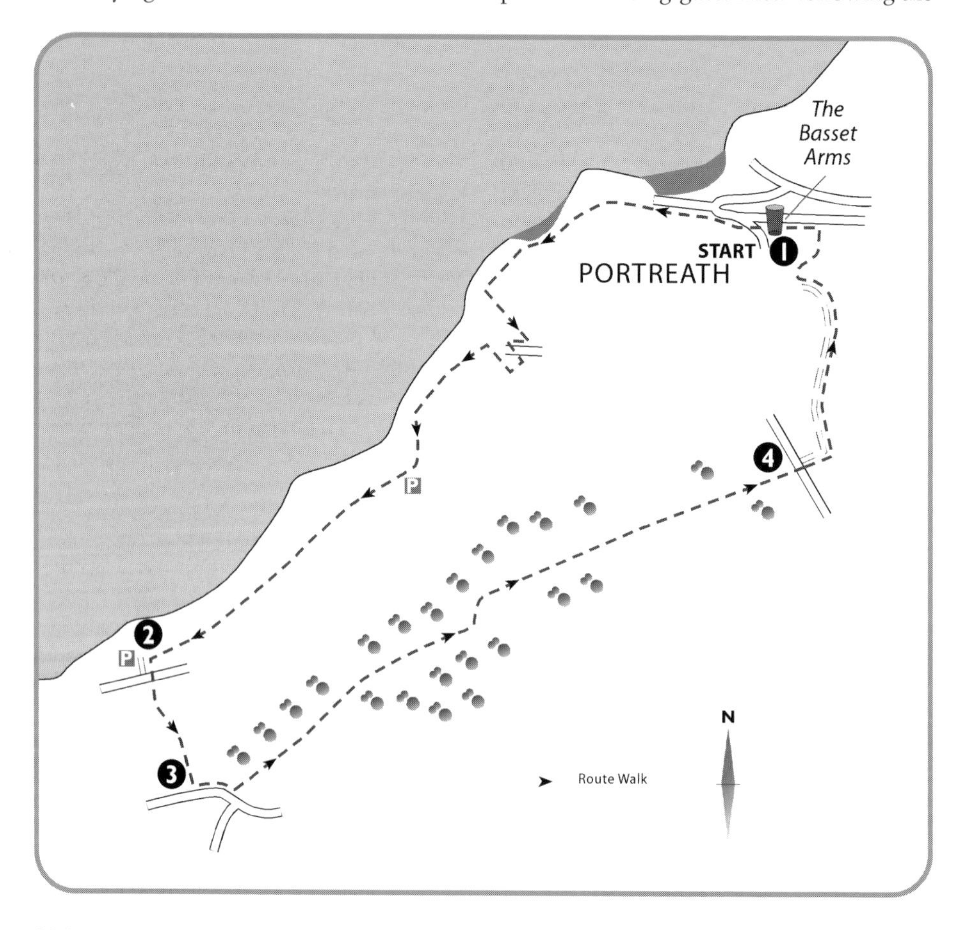

cliff for 600 yards you go through a second kissing-gate, and after a further $^1/_2$ mile through a third, which brings you to another car park. *(3 miles)*

2 Turn left and follow a track to a road; cross straight over to a stile. Keep to the left of the field on the other side. The path eventually runs between high hedges, and you emerge through a gate onto another road. *($^1/_2$ mile)*

3 Turn left and after a couple of hundred yards, as the road swings right, turn left up a short drive. This leads onto a broad path and into the lovely mixed woodland of Tehidy Country Park, which stretches for almost 2 miles ahead. When you come to a junction, with a path going right to Oak Wood, go straight on (signposted to Otter Bridge). At the next junction, where the path forks, go left to climb slightly and join a track. Turn left and climb a short hill to another junction. Turn right (signposted to East Lodge). You pass an estate of houses on the right and then re-enter the wood.

At the path junction just beyond the houses go straight on, and at the next junction straight on again (still signposted to East Lodge). You will see a golf course through the trees on the right. Turn right at the T-junction and go through two kissing-gates in quick succession as you cross one of the tees. The path now runs alongside the golf course. At the end it re-enters the wood and about 50 yards further on you will find a path going left. Take it and at the first two forks follow the main path to the left. It brings you out at a car park. *(2 miles)*

4 Leave the car park via the vehicle entrance and turn right along the road beyond. After a few yards turn left along a broad green lane. After a while it narrows and swings left. It broadens to a farm track and soon you will see Portreath ahead, with the sea beyond. You come to a T-junction at the outbuildings of Duchy College; go left and after 50 yards right. When the track ends, turn left along a path, following the public footpath sign. It swings to the right and after a few yards you will see another public footpath sign pointing left; go down there.

After some steps you come to a junction, where a path goes left to cross a bridge; carry straight on. The path descends to the outskirts of Portreath, where you join a lane. Go straight on and at the junction turn left. You will come to a sign saying 'No vehicle access'; go straight on and when the road ends join a path. The Basset Arms is on the left. *(1 mile)*

Date walk completed:

....

Places of Interest Nearby

About $2^1/_2$ miles away, on the way to Redruth, is **Cornish Goldsmiths**. Telephone: 01209 218198. Five miles away at Pool, is the National Trust's **Cornish Mines and Engines**. Telephone: 01209 315027.

Walk **34** *Malpas*

The Heron Inn

Malpas lies at the confluence of two large tidal rivers – the Truro and the Tresillian – that feed into the Fal estuary, a site of great natural interest and home to a wide variety of birds. This walk follows both of them. You go up the Truro to the city of the same name before taking a lane through countryside and woodland to join the Tresillian. You then return to Malpas along this river, often with a wealth of wild flowers alongside the path.

***Distance:** 6 miles*

OS Explorer 105 Falmouth and Mevagissey
GR 844427

A moderate to easy walk along mainly flat terrain, with just one hill

Starting point: The Heron Inn. Please do not leave your car in the car park while walking. There is parking in the road (but park with care, as the lane is narrow and a large bus has to pass). If you prefer, you can park in Truro and start the walk at point 2 (using the Viaduct pay and display car park).

How to get there: Turn south from the A390 at the large Trafalgar roundabout in Truro, following the sign for Malpas.

Dating back to the 19th century, the delightful **Heron Inn** comprises one long room divided into four sections: a slate-floored bar, a snug alcove behind it and wooden-floored eating areas on either side. There are two stone fireplaces, and the whole place has a light, airy atmosphere. Outside, on the opposite side of the lane, there is a terrace overlooking the river. The menu ranges from rolls and tortilla wraps, through omelettes and pasta to steaks and specials such as pork in cider gravy and barbecued chicken fillets. The Heron is particularly renowned, however, for its fresh local fish, especially crab.

***Telephone:** 01872 272773.*

The Walk

❶ Turn right from the pub and follow the lane out of Malpas. After 500 yards or so go down some steps by a bench on the left and follow a path between the lane and the river, in amongst trees. When the path meets the lane again, turn sharp left down steps to the water's edge, and at the bottom turn right along a concrete path. Where this joins the lane, bear left. The lane ends at the large Trafalgar roundabout; turn right. *(1¾ miles)*

❷ Take the next turning on the right, up St Clement's Hill. Follow this road, ignoring turnings to left and right, as it climbs steadily through the suburbs of Truro. At the top, you pass a school and the road narrows to a lane. Follow its undulations. It descends through dense woodland, curving to the right and to the left, and passes some houses. Just beyond the houses it crosses a stream and goes up to a main road. Just before the stream, turn right up the drive for Pencalenick School. *(1¾ miles)*

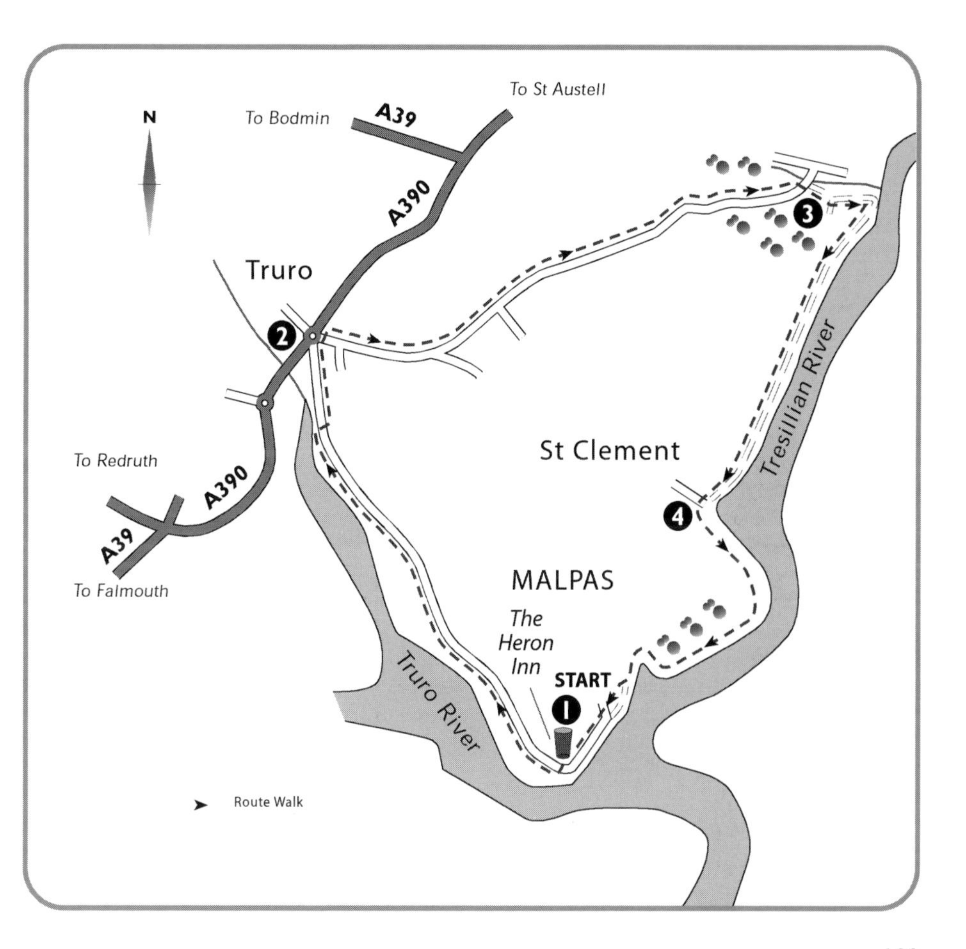

Truro cathedral

❸ As the drive bends sharply to the right, bear left along a track, following the stream. You will pass a marsh on the left and then come to the Tresillian River. The track swings right to follow it downstream. After about ½ mile you pass Tresemple Pond on the right, and then after another ½ mile you go through a gate onto a track, which leads to a lane at St Clement. *(1½ miles)*

❹ Just beyond the parking area, turn left along a path, which is marked as Denas Road. This takes you through a wood, with glimpses of the river alongside you. You leave the wood via a stile; keep to the left of a field to a ladder stile. Keep to the left again and cross another stile into another wood. Climb some steps on the right, away from the river for a short distance, and then go down some more to rejoin it. Some more steps follow as you skirt an inlet. Cross a stile and go down some more steps. At the path junction, turn left, following the public footpath sign for Malpas. Cross a small stream and go through a kissing-gate. Follow the path on the other side to a lane; bear right. At the next junction bear left and follow this lane back to the Heron Inn. *(1 mile)*

Date walk completed:

Places of Interest Nearby

Truro is on the route of this walk. Among the attractions there are the **cathedral** and the **Royal Cornwall Museum**. Telephone: 01872 272205.

Pentewan

The Ship Inn

For interest and variety, this walk is hard to beat: tracks that are fringed with flowers for much of the year, woods, coastal paths, the lovely fishing village of Mevagissey, and the chance to visit the fascinating and beautiful Lost Gardens of Heligan along the way. The views are outstanding, both along the coast and inland.

Distance: *5½ miles*

OS Explorer 105 Falmouth and Mevagissey
GR 018473

A moderate to challenging walk, with two steep hills to negotiate, one at the start and another about halfway round.

Starting point: The free car park in Pentewan. The pub has no car park.

How to get there: Turn south onto the B3273 off the A390 at St Austell, following the signs for Mevagissey. After 3 miles, Pentewan is signposted off to the left. The car park is on the right just beyond a sharp right-hand bend, and the pub about 100 yards further, on the left.

The **Ship Inn** is a warm, welcoming pub, full of character and atmosphere. There are solid oak beams and pillars, and it is carpeted throughout. The small public bar has a games room off the side, and there is a large lounge and dining area, the latter on two levels with a balustrade. Both have stone fireplaces. A large garden lies across the road, alongside the mouth of the St Austell River. The pub prides itself on its local real ales, while the food menu ranges from filled baguettes and salads to a variety of meat and vegetarian specials and fresh fish.

Telephone: 01726 842855.

The Walk

❶ Turn left out of the car park and follow the road you came in on as it swings left to cross the St Austell River. It comes out onto the B3273; turn right and follow it for a short distance until you see two tracks on the left. Take the second one, which climbs up the hill. There is a public footpath sign, but it is somewhat hidden by the trees. Go through a kissing-gate and follow the track round to the right, still climbing. As you emerge into a field, follow the track round to the left and go through another kissing-gate into a field; keep to the left.

At the end, go through the right-hand of two gateways, and keep to the left of the field beyond. Go through another three gateways and straight across the fields in between. Cross a third field to a gate and keep to the right of the final field. About halfway along the hedge you will find a stile on the right, leading into a wood. Keep to the left-hand edge and leave the wood via another stile on the

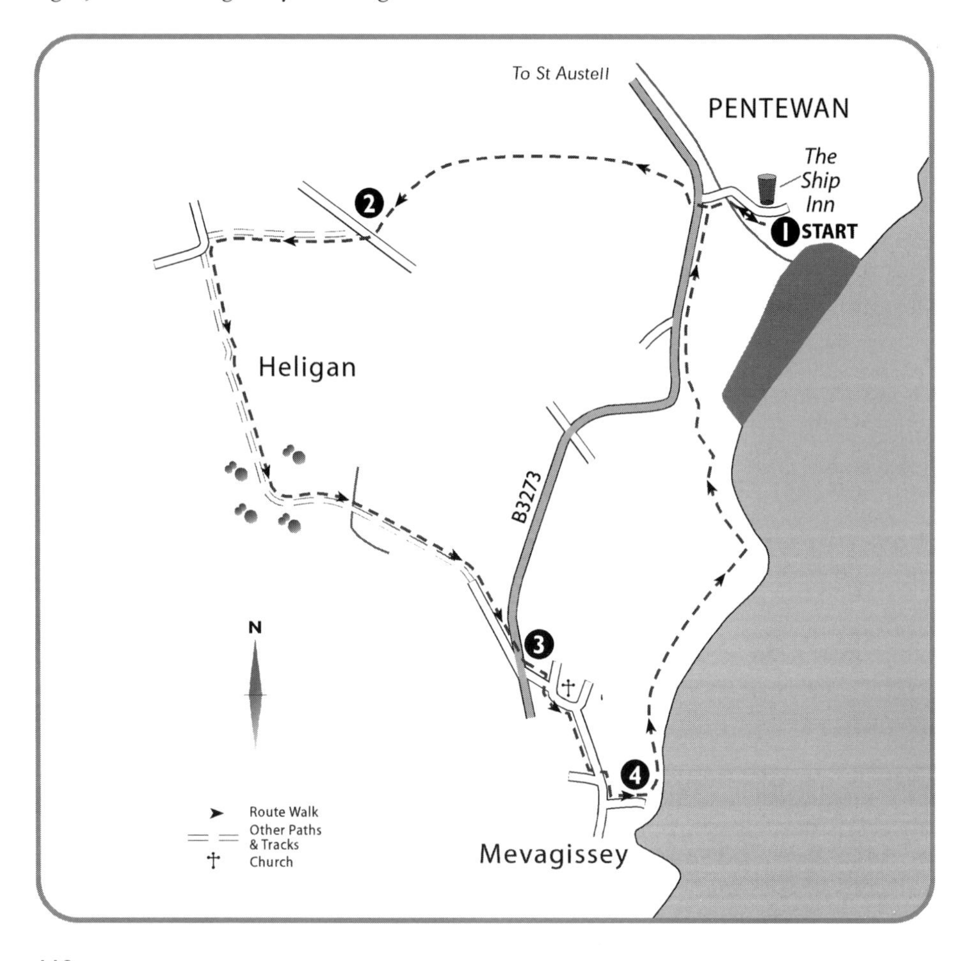

left. Bear right between a hedge and a high bank. Cross a third stile through the wood to a road. *(1¼ miles)*

❷ Cross the road and follow the clear path on the other side. Where it forks, go right, following the sign for Pentewan. When it swings sharp right you will see a gate ahead of you with a sign indicating that this is a permissive path to Heligan Wood. Cross the stile alongside it and follow the track. You emerge onto the drive of a campsite; go straight on, and when you come to the Warden's Lodge pass it and turn right. At the main road turn left and cross the entrance to Heligan Gardens. Go straight on to a track marked with a public footpath sign.

At the crossroads go straight on, and straight on again at the pedestrian crossing from the car park to the gardens. The track descends steeply to cross a stream. Turn sharp right, following the sign for Mevagissey. Cross a stile, ignore the next and continue along the broad path. Go through a gate and along a track above a stream. Go through a gateway, cross a small stream to a surfaced lane. This comes out at the B3273 on the edge of Mevagissey. *(1¾ miles)*

❸ Cross straight over and follow the road on the other side. At the T-junction turn right. At the next T-junction bear right and at the next go straight on to the centre of the village. When you get to the post office, go left to the harbour. Go along the left-hand side of the quay. *(½ mile)*

❹ You will see a steep path going up the hill, signposted as the Coast Path to Pentewan. Follow that up above the harbour. There are then some steps. Cross a grassy stretch with a children's playground at the top. At the far end, join a surfaced path along the top of the cliff. As you leave the houses you cross a stone stile and go down into a valley. At the bottom, cross a footbridge and go left to climb the steep hill opposite. Go through a kissing-gate into a field and continue to climb.

At the top of the field cross a stile; there is now a hedge and then a fence between you and the field on your left. Cross another stile onto a track, which leads you into another field. After another stile you can look down on Sconhoe and Pentewan beaches. Cross another stile and go down a steep hill. The path swings left to cross a stile, then two more separated by a footbridge. Turn right on the other side and climb a short hill. Two more stiles follow in quick succession. You go through a small copse, then rejoin the road and finally come to the entrance to Pentewan Sands Holiday Park. Continue on the pavement alongside the main road for a couple of hundred yards to the turning to Pentewan on the right. Follow the lane round to the right to the village, the car park and the pub. *(2 miles)*

Date walk completed:

....

Places of Interest Nearby

About ½ mile from Helford Passage, across the ferry from Helford, is **Trebah** (telephone 01326 250448), and a little further on **Glendurgan** (telephone 01326 250906), two lovely gardens overlooking the river (the latter a National Trust property).

36 St Mawes

The Idle Rocks Hotel

The Roseland Peninsula is noted as one of the loveliest areas in Cornwall, and this splendid route will show you why. It takes you from the pretty fishing village of St Mawes up the Percuil River, with good views upstream. It then cuts inland to join a path along the ridge of the peninsula, where the views across Carrick Roads will take your breath away. There is a chance to visit the churchyard at St Just in Roseland, probably the most beautiful churchyard in the South-West, before you return to St Mawes along Carrick Roads itself and past Henry VIII's castle.

Distance: *5¼ miles*

OS Explorer 105 Falmouth and Mevagissey
GR 848331

A fairly easy walk along generally easy terrain but with one muddy stretch after rain

Starting point: The pay and display car park in St Mawes, almost opposite the Idle Rocks Hotel. The hotel itself has no parking.

How to get there: St Mawes is at the end of the A3078, which runs south from the A390 Truro to St Austell road. The car park is on the right in the middle of the village and is clearly marked. The Idle Rocks Hotel is on the left.

The **Idle Rocks Hotel** is an elegant, comfortable establishment, with a position that makes it the ideal choice for a drink or a meal after your walk. Set right on the edge of the harbour, the views from the bar and terrace are stunning. Beyond the bar is the brasserie, which enjoys similar views. There is also a more formal restaurant. The place to be on a sunny summer's day, however, is on the terrace, which is perched just above the rocks. Local fish is a speciality of the bar menu, but the fare also ranges from sandwiches and ploughman's lunches to salads and steaks.

Telephone: 01326 270771.

The Walk

1 Turn left as you leave the car park and follow the road as it hugs St Mawes Harbour. The road swings to the left and you will find Polvarth Lane on your right; turn down it. At the bottom you will see a footpath going left just above the quay, pointing to Porthcuil Creek; take it. *(½ mile)*

2 The path swings left around a boatyard. You come to a lane; turn right and just before you reach the boatyard turn left, following the large, red public footpath sign. Leaving the houses behind you cross a stile into a field above a small bay. Keep right initially, and when you come to a large tree standing on its own swing left up the field to follow the path between bushes.

Where it forks go left and you will soon emerge into a field. Go straight across to a gate and straight across the next field. At the end of the field turn right and follow the hedge to a gate, which leads onto a green lane (which can become muddy). This broadens to a track

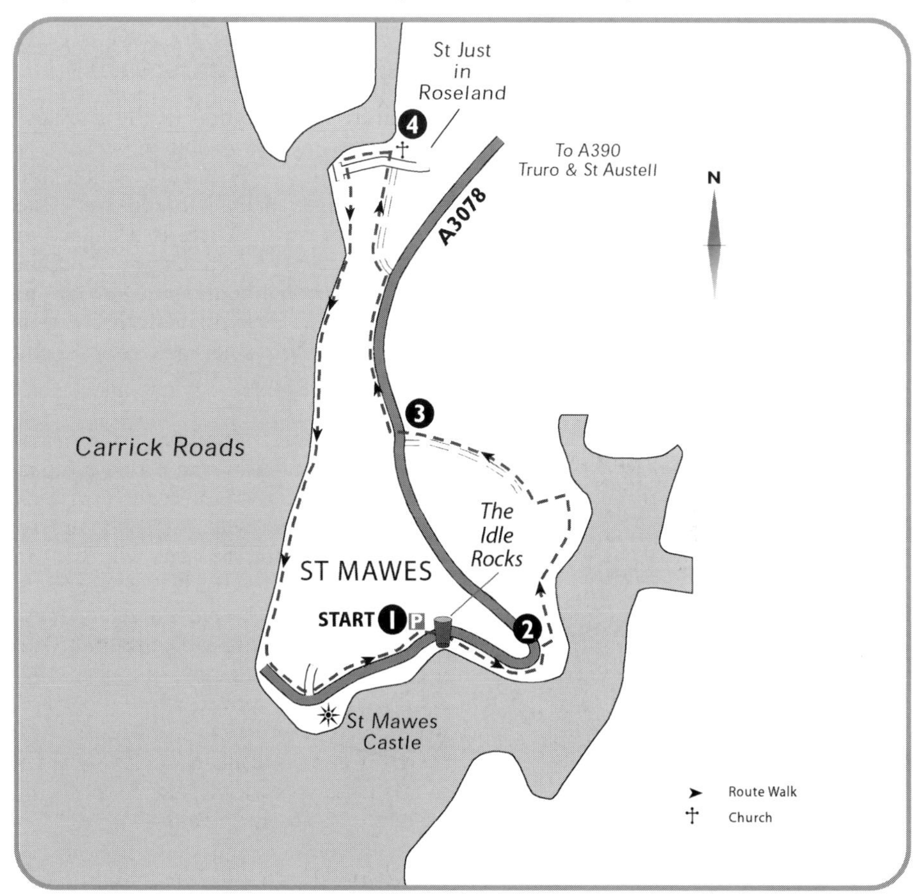

and goes through a gate. A little further on two more gates take you into a farmyard. When you get to the track junction, go left and through another gate. The track comes out at the main road; turn right. *(1¼ miles)*

❸ After a few yards you will see a gap in the hedge on the left; turn off the road here and immediately right across a stile, following the National Trust footpath sign for St Just. Cross four fields separated by stiles, keeping to the right all the time. You then go through a gap in a hedge and another stile takes you into a green lane; turn left. The green lane comes out into a field; keep to the left and after a while the path becomes a green lane again and begins to descend gently to some houses. Cross a drive to some steps; at the bottom turn left and you will come out into a lane; turn left again and almost immediately right into the delightful and peaceful churchyard on a hillside overlooking St Just Creek. *(1 mile)*

❹ Follow the path down to the church and turn left. Leave the churchyard via a gate and follow the path past some boathouses. It comes out at a lane. At the junction turn right, following the public footpath sign for St Mawes. Just before the lane ends at a house turn left through a gate (signposted as a public footpath to St Mawes). Turn immediately right along the edge of the field. At the end go through another gate and turn right and then left to go round the edge of the next field.

St Mawes castle

You now cross several fields, separated by a succession of gates and stiles, keeping to the right all the time and ignoring the odd gate or stile on the right leading down to the water. After 1¾ miles you go through a gate onto a road past some houses. It bears left and climbs behind the Tudor St Mawes Castle and then descends into St Mawes. Follow the harbour round and after ½ mile or so you will find the car park on the left and the Idle Rocks Hotel just beyond it on the right. *(2½ miles)*

Date walk completed:

....

Places of Interest Nearby

St Mawes Castle built by Henry VIII as a defence against the French (English Heritage). Telephone: 01326 270526. Five miles to the north of St Mawes you can take the King Harry ferry to the National Trust's **Trelissick Garden**. Telephone: 01872 862090.

Ludgvan 37

The White Hart

St Michael's Way is part of a network of pilgrim routes leading to Santiago de Compostela in Spain. It runs from Lelant in the north to Marazion in the south, passing through Ludgvan. This walk follows the Way north mainly along farm paths and green lanes, returning to Ludgvan along green lanes and lanes. There are some outstanding views, with St Michael's Mount and the bay of Gwavas Lake prominent for much of the time, and an array of summer flowers along the way.

Distance: *4¼ miles*

OS Explorer 102 Land's End
GR 506330

A moderate walk, with just a couple of hills, one fairly steep

Starting point: The White Hart. The landlady has no objection to customers leaving their cars in the car park in the morning if they are returning for lunch, but please do not park there if you are walking over the lunch period. There is more parking in the road.

How to get there: The village is about ¾ mile west of the A30 just north of Penzance, and is signposted. The White Hart is next to the church.

The **White Hart** is a lovely 14th-century inn, originally built to house the men working on the church. It is a warm, cosy place with a low ceiling, dark beams and thick dark walls decorated with a variety of knick-knacks and old paintings. The long bar has a wooden floor with rugs and there are several little snugs off it, separated by wooden panelling; one of these has an enormous granite fireplace. The menu is wide ranging, from snacks such as sandwiches and pasties to steaks, fish dishes and a variety of mouthwatering daily specials. Food is not served on Mondays, however.

Telephone: *01736 740574.*

The Walk

❶ Turn right and walk past the church. Just beyond it turn right again up a track, signposted with the St Michael's Way waymark, a stylised scallop shell. At the junction after a few yards go straight on along the main track. After a while the track ends; continue along the path that runs straight on into a wood. It descends and at the bottom crosses a small stream and a stile. Cross the field on the other side to another stile, which leads into a green lane. It takes you up a hill, through a gate and onto a lane.

Turn left, and after 150 yards right through a gap in a hedge, following the public footpath sign. Keep to the left of the field on the other side and you get a lovely view to the right. Cross a stile at the end and follow the path on the other side, which goes diagonally across a long field. Follow the right-hand boundary to a stile leading into a small wood. The

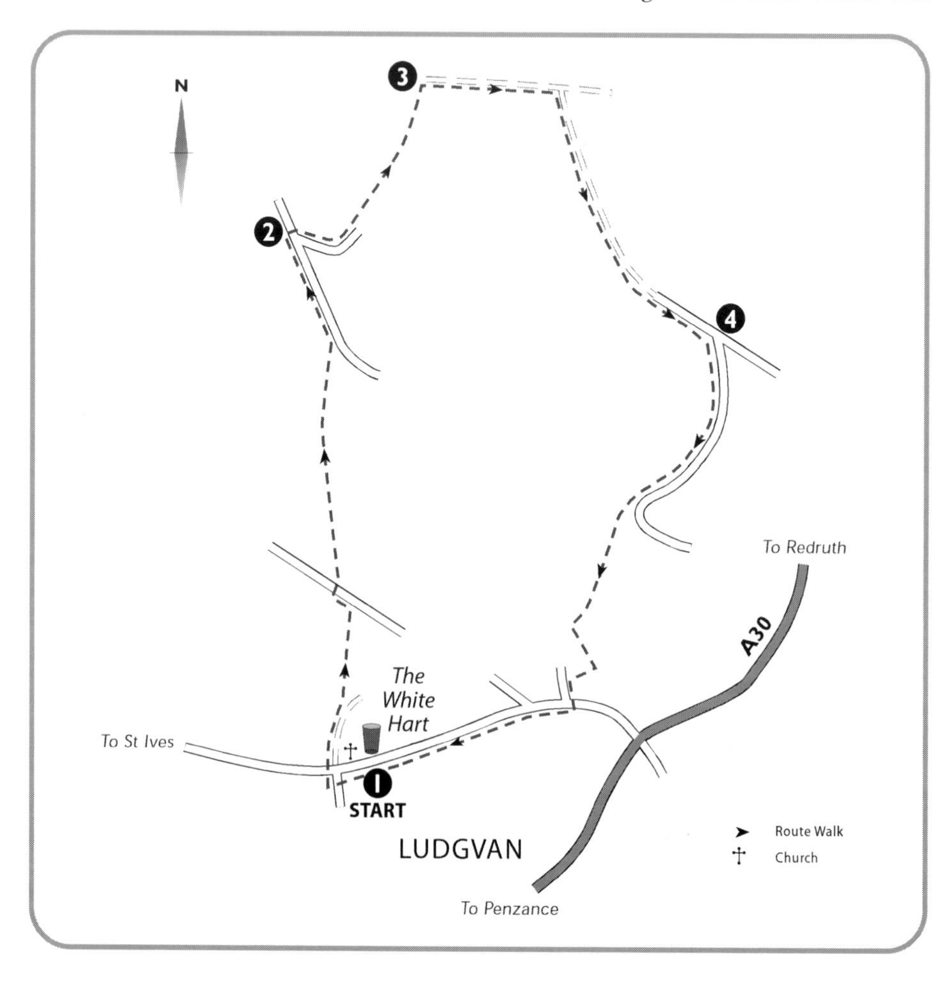

path takes you to a stone footbridge followed by a stile. Bear left on the other side to another stile and go diagonally left across the next field. Looking back now you get a good view of St Michael's Mount. Go up some steps to the left of a gate and keep to the left of the next field. Cross another stile into a lane and go straight on. *(1 mile)*

2 After ¼ mile you come to a junction; turn sharp right down a hill. Go down to a ford with a footbridge alongside it. Just beyond it, you will come to a track leading through a gate on the left; cross the stile alongside the gate and follow the track to the next gate. Go round to the left of that, along a path leading to a stile. Climb steeply through the trees and gorse on the other side to another stile. Keep to the right of a field, still climbing but more gently now. You get a good view behind you and to your right, and soon to your left as well. Cross a stile and bear left across the next field, with the bulk of Trencrom Hill ahead of you. Cross two stiles and cross the next field to yet another stile leading into a green lane; turn right, leaving the route of St Michael's Way. *(¾ mile)*

3 After following this pretty green lane between high hedges for about 250 yards you will come to a junction, with another green lane going off to the right; go straight on. After another 200 yards turn right through a gate along a broad track. Soon you get another extensive view to your left. You pass some farm buildings and another panorama comes into view ahead of you. You pass a farm and come out at a surfaced lane. Follow it for ¼ mile to a fork and go right. *(1 mile)*

4 Soon St Michael's Mount comes into sight again, and this time you get another fine view round Gwavas Lake, past Penzance. After 600 yards, as the lane turns sharp left, go straight on down a track. After a short distance, when the track swings right to some houses, go straight on along a path, down some steps and through a barrier. Keep to the left, cross a stone stile at the end of the field and keep to the left again beyond it. Towards the bottom of the next field go through a gate and follow the path on the other side as it descends steeply through some trees.

At the bottom, cross a track to a gate. Bear left on the other side to a footbridge. Go straight across on the other side to some steps and a kissing-gate. Turn left beyond that and follow a path to a track. At the fork go right and at the junction with a road go left. At the next T-junction turn right, and follow this road up a hill for about ½ mile and you will find the pub on your right. Towards the top of the hill, look left for a last view of St Michael's Mount. *(1½ miles)*

Date walk completed:

....

Places of Interest Nearby

Just 2½ miles from Ludgvan is **St Michael's Mount** (National Trust). Telephone: 01736 710507. It is crowned by a medieval castle and church. At St Ives, about 6 miles to the north, is the **Tate St Ives**. Telephone: 01736 796226.

Walk 38 Lamorna

The Lamorna Wink

Stunning coastal views and quiet lanes and paths are the main feature of this walk. You climb out of Lamorna and follow a pretty lane through rich farmland before descending to the South West Coast Path just south of Mousehole. This path takes you to Lamorna Cove, a delightful little backwater.

Distance: *4 miles*

OS Explorer 102 Land's End
GR 446245

A fairly challenging walk, with a steep climb near the start and one or two more towards the end, as well as some rocks to negotiate

Starting point: The Lamorna Wink. Customers can leave their cars in the pub car park while they walk, but please ask first. There is also a public car park at Lamorna Cove.

How to get there: Turn south off the B3315 between Penzance and Land's End, following the sign for Lamorna Cove. The pub is on the left through the village.

The **Lamorna Wink** derives its strange name from the Beer Act of 1830, which allowed any householder to apply for a beer licence. These establishments were called kiddleywinks, soon shortened to 'winks'. This is a fascinating hostelry. The dark bar is filled with seafaring memorabilia, while alongside there is a quiet, light lounge, with shelves of books. Outside there is an attractive lawned area. The food is simple, home-made bar fare and includes sandwiches, pasties, jacket potatoes, ploughman's lunches and salads.

Telephone: *01736 731566.*

The Walk

❶ Turn right as you leave the pub, and almost immediately right again along a lane. It goes down a hill to cross a stream, and then climbs steeply up the other side of the valley. It swings to the right and then the left, still climbing, and then levels off. This is a most attractive stretch, with hedgerows full of spring flowers on either side, and almost total silence all around. You pass some houses and a farm, and just beyond them you will see a public footpath sign on the left; climb some steps to a gate. *(3/4 mile)*

❷ Turn right immediately beyond the gate to follow the right-hand edge of a field, alongside the lane. You get a good view from here out to sea on the right. Cross a stone stile at the end of the field and keep to the right again. At the end of the next field a gate leads back onto the lane. After 50 yards you will see another

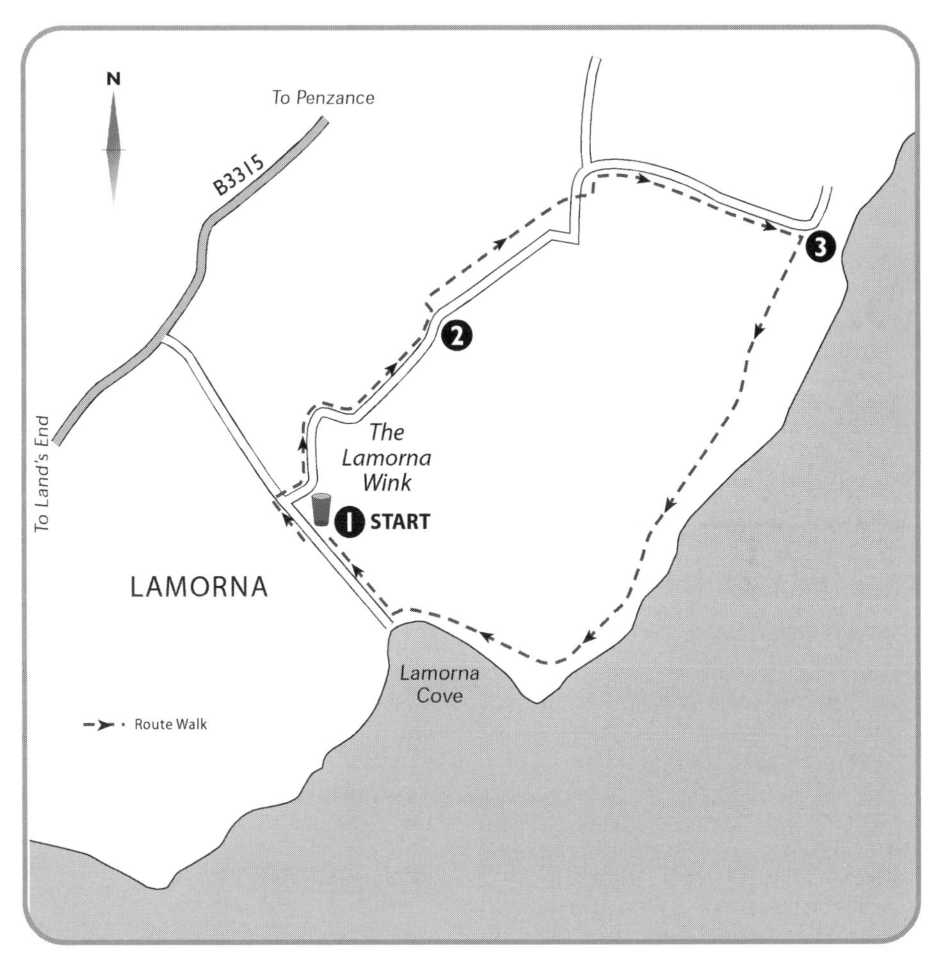

The old mill at Lamorna

public footpath on the left. Cross a stone stile and keep to the right of the field beyond. At the end cross two stone stiles in quick succession and keep to the right of the next field again. You now get a superb view over the rolling farmland to the left.

At the end go through a gate and onto the lane again. After about 100 yards you will come to a junction; turn right (signposted to Raginnis and Mousehole). You soon get a lovely view out to sea and round Mount's Bay ahead of you. You pass some houses and begin to descend. As the lane begins to swing to the left, just beyond the 20 mph sign, you will see a track on the right, marked with a Coast Path sign; turn off here. *(1 mile)*

❸ Follow the track between some houses, and continue as it narrows to a broad path. There is an abundance of wild flowers along here in season, including some exquisite, deep red fuchsias. The path opens up on the left and there is another excellent view back around Mount's May, dominated by St Michael's Mount. You pass an old blockhouse, and the path descends. It swings left down some steps and runs just above the rocks. You cross a small stream and the path passes among another mass of fuchsias. All this time it is climbing steadily, but in stages, away from the rocks.

The path enters a belt of trees and then opens out again, before swinging right up some steep steps. At the top you are rewarded with an encouraging view ahead to Lamorna Cove. The path twists and winds among the rocks of a headland and comes out at a bridge across a stream at the cove. Cross it and pass some houses to the public car park. Turn right and follow the lane as it climbs up to the pub. *(2¼ miles)*

Date walk completed:

....

Places of Interest Nearby

Four miles away, in Newlyn, is the **Pilchard Works**, with exhibits, demonstrations and activities. Telephone: 01736 332112. About the same distance in the other direction is the **Porthcurno Telegraph Museum**. Telephone: 01736 810966.

Helford 39

The Shipwright's Arms

This lovely route combines woodland and riverside paths with the chance to enjoy some stunning coastal views. You start with a brief exploration of the delightful village of Helford, and then follow a wooded valley and farm paths to Manaccan. Another woodland path takes you to the pretty Gillan Creek – a haven for water birds – and you follow this almost to the sea. After rounding Dennis Head, from where you have superb views along the coast in both directions, the path takes you back along the mouth of the Helford River, with more woods along the way.

Distance: *5 miles*

OS Explorer 103 The Lizard
GR 759260 (car park) 758262 (pub)

A moderate walk along clear paths, with just one or two climbs

Starting point: The public pay and display car park at the entrance to Helford. The pub car park is very small, and not suitable for walkers' cars.

How to get there: Take the A3083 south from Helston and turn off left onto the B3293. Take the second left, following the signs to Mawgan, and you will find Helford signposted from there. Alternatively, you can take the pedestrian ferry from Helford Passage.

The cosy old **Shipwright's Arms** is perched on the very edge of the Helford River, with lovely views down to the sea. It comprises just the one bar, which is on two levels, its stone walls decorated with a nautical theme – old photographs, displays of knots, navigation lamps and model ships – and the board ceiling has coins sunk into it. Outside there is a riverside terrace. At lunchtime the food ranges from soup and ploughman's lunches to a variety of salads, while in the evening there is a more extensive menu, including garlic mushrooms, smoked mackerel and steaks. Local fish is, of course, a speciality.

Telephone: 01326 231235.

The Walk

❶ Turn right from the car park and follow the road down into the village. At the bottom, go right for the Shipwright's Arms, which is about 1/4 mile further on, or left up a concrete track for the walk (signposted as the footpath to Manaccan). At the top go straight on along a broad path, continuing past a junction. Cross a small footbridge. At the next junction, follow the path round to the left. After a few yards there is another junction; go straight on.

A stone stile takes you out of the wood and into a field; keep to the left. Follow the path round to the right and then to the left at the end. A few yards after turning left, go right across the field to a gate and a stile leading into a lane. Turn left and then almost immediately right across a stone stile into another field. Keep left and at the end follow a path between fences to a stone stile and a

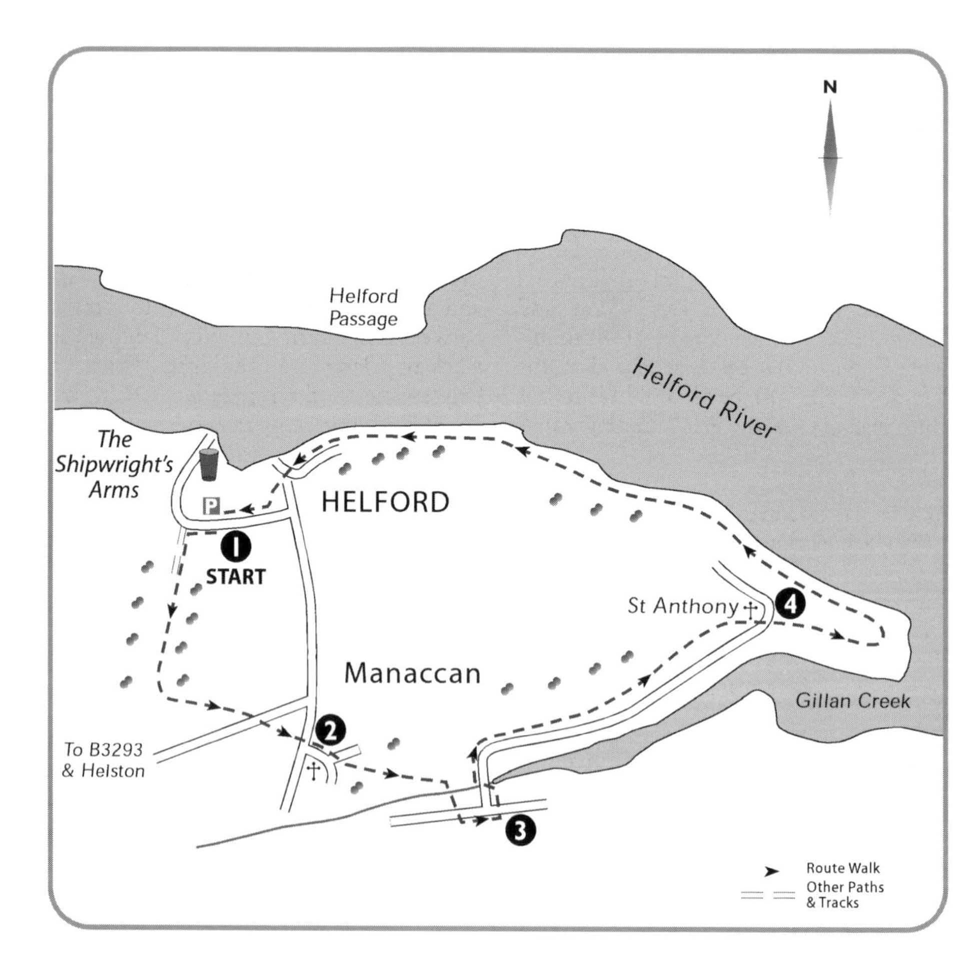

road; go straight on and at the T-junction turn right into Manaccan. *(1¼ miles)*

❷ After 50 yards or so you will come to a pub on the left; turn left just before it and follow the lane to the right round a church. On the bend, turn left down another lane, following the public footpath sign. After 100 yards turn right down a track (signposted as a public footpath to Carne). Cross a stone stile and keep to the right of a field. Cross another stone stile and keep to the right again. At the end cross yet another stone stile to enter a wood. The path descends through the wood and emerges onto a lane; turn left. After 150 yards you come to a junction; turn left again. *(½ mile)*

❸ Cross a bridge and follow the lane as it swings to the right to follow Gillan Creek. It then climbs slightly away from the creek, enters a pretty wood and continues to the hamlet of St Anthony, where you follow the lane round to the left up a hill. Just beyond a gate to the churchyard take the path leading right. *(1 mile)*

❹ After a few yards you come to a track with a Coast Path sign pointing right to Helford; follow it up through a kissing-gate and continue along the track as it crosses a field. At the end follow the path through some bushes. Cross the stile on your left and continue to Dennis Head. Around the headland and you will come to a T-junction; go right and cross a stile back into the field you came out of. Turn right and follow the right-hand edge of the field. (If you wish you can turn left as you enter the field and avoid the circuit of Dennis Head, but you will miss the marvellous views.)

At the end you will come to a kissing-gate; follow the path along the edge of the field beyond. Go through a gap in the bank and keep to the right again. Cross a stone stile and again keep to the right. Another stone stile takes you into another field. You soon leave the field via a kissing-gate on the right. Go left along a path between hedges.

After a while the path descends into a wood and around a small cove. It climbs slightly on the other side; at the junction just above the cove go sharp right. You descend again to a kissing-gate and another cove and continue to a track between some farm buildings. Follow the track to a lane and bear right. When the lane swings to the right after 100 yards, go left up some steps and follow the path at the top. Soon you will see the car park on your right, with a gate leading through to it. *(2¼ miles)*

Date walk completed:

....

Places of Interest Nearby

About ½ mile from Helford Passage, across the ferry from Helford, are two lovely gardens: **Trebah** (telephone: 01326 250448), and **Glendurgan** (telephone: 01326 250906). The **National Seal Sanctuary** is 8 miles west at Gweek. Telephone: 01326 221874.

Walk 40 The Lizard

The Top House

This walk gives you an opportunity to walk to the most southerly point in England, and to enjoy some excellent coastal views along the way. You can also visit Kynance Cove, a delightful inlet with rock pools and a lovely little beach. Apart from the Coast Path, where there are a few hills to climb, the route mainly follows easy tracks and paths. An added advantage is that, if you would like a shorter walk, there are a number of short cuts back to the village from the Coast Path.

Distance: *4½ miles*

OS Explorer 103 The Lizard
GR 703125

A moderate walk along easy paths with just a few climbs in the middle

Starting point: The Top House. There is roadside parking nearby.

How to get there: Take the A3083 south from Helston. Lizard is at the end of the road, and the pub is on The Square in the centre of the village.

The **Top House,** a converted farmhouse that has been a pub for 200 years, has a cosy atmosphere. It is decorated with an interesting array of seafaring memorabilia, and two of the seats in the bar came from a wreck. The lounge, which is carpeted, displays a number of original watercolours. The bar has a parquet floor and an open fireplace and there is a patio outside. The food is good pub fare: sandwiches, jacket potatoes, ploughman's lunches, pies, fish and steaks. Fresh local produce is used wherever possible, including locally caught fish and locally reared meat.

Telephone: *01326 290974.*

The Walk

❶ Turn left as you leave the pub, and at the crossroads after a few yards go straight across (signposted to Kynance Cove). You pass some houses and the road becomes a track. Soon after it does so it forks; go right (still signposted to Kynance Cove). When it goes right into a field bear left, following the footpath sign. Go up some steps and along the top of a bank. At the end go down some steps and into a belt of trees. You soon emerge into an area of gorse and bramble and cross a stile. You now get a good view out to sea on the left. Cross another stile and bear right across a field. At the end cross another stile to a surfaced road; go straight on.

This area is a mass of heather in different shades of purple in summer, interspersed with the yellow of gorse. You come out at a National Trust car park. Here you can either turn left through a gap in a wall to join the Coast Path or right to cross the car park and go down to Kynance Cove – a lovely place to stop for a break and, in my view,

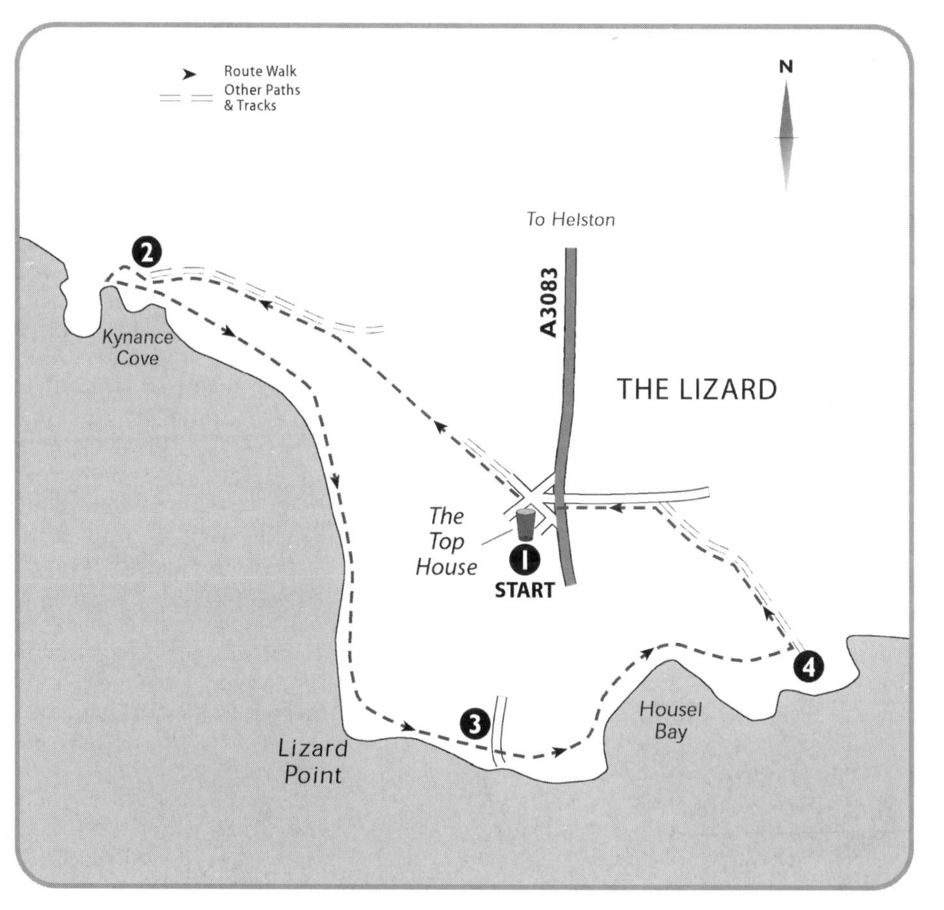

worth a visit. However, if you do go down to it you will have a fairly steep climb up some steps back to the cliff top. *(1 1/4 miles)*

Kynance Cove

❷ As you follow the Coast Path past the car park you get a very good view along the coast ahead of you. You will see various paths going off to the left; ignore these and continue along the main path near the cliff edge. You go round Pentreath Beach, above which is a stone stile followed shortly by another one. A few yards after the second one you will see a wooden stile on the right; cross it and go down some steps. After a short level stretch you go down some more steps to cross two streams. More steps take you steeply up the other side and you go through a gap in a wall. After about 1/2 mile you go through another gap in a wall and soon round Lizard Point. Go down some steps to cross a small stream and you will shortly pass some houses and a café and come to a road. Turn right and then left into a car park. You are now at the southernmost point in England. *(1 1/2 miles)*

❸ Go through the car park and onto the path on the other side. You pass the Lizard lighthouse and the path swings left round Housel Bay. It descends steeply to cross a stream and then climbs steeply up the other side again. At the junction in the path go round to the right, following the Coast Path's acorn waymark. You pass in front of the Housel Bay Hotel and then come to the Lizard Wireless Station, which dates back to 1901 and is looked after by the National Trust. Just beyond it, and before you come to the Lloyds Signal Station, bear left off the Coast Path along a track to a gate. *(1 mile)*

❹ Turn left beyond the gate along another track and follow it as it winds through the fields. It comes out at a farm and a road on the edge of the village. Turn left and follow the road to the centre of the village and the Top House. *(3/4 mile)*

Date walk completed:

....

Places of Interest Nearby

The **Lizard Wireless Station**, passed on the walk, has limited opening times and is only accessible on foot. Telephone: 01326 290384. However, about 8 miles north of the Lizard is the **Goonhilly Satellite Earth Station**, the largest in the world. Telephone: 01872 325400. Ten miles away, on the outskirts of Helston, is **Flambards** theme park. Telephone 0845 6018684.